AF646614

Rajiv Gandhi's Vision on Local Governance

ABOUT THE AUTHOR

Prof. Ganapathi Palanithurai, Coordinator in Rajiv Gandhi Chair, Gandhigram Rural Institute, presently heads the Department of Political Science and Development Administration, Gandhigram Rural University, Tamil Nadu. He is also associated with Central Planning Commission, State Planning Commission of Tamil Nadu, Population Foundation of India, the Ford Foundation, UNICEF, Rajiv Gandhi Foundation, CAPART, Ministry of Rural Development and DANIDA (Danish-Indo Development Agency) in specific areas of activities in connection with empowerment of people.

Prof. Palanithurai has to his credit fifty-two books and ninty-five articles on three major areas, namely, legislative behaviour, ethnicity and Panchayati Raj system. He was recipient of Fellowship from Sastri Indo-Canadian Institute, New Delhi and World Academy of Art and Science, USA. He is the Chairman of the Tamil Nadu Council for Sustainable Livelihoods. He was a visiting Fellow in the MiGill University, Canada in 1989. He is a member of the expert committee constituted by the Government of Tamil Nadu to monitor the training programme for local body leaders. He is a member of High Level Committee headed by the Minister of Panchayati Raj, Government of Tamil Nadu for further devolution of powers.

Rajiv Gandhi's Vision on Local Governance

G. PALANITHURAI

CONCEPT PUBLISHING COMPANY, NEW DELHI-110059

© Author

All rights reserved. No part of this work may be reproduced, stored, adapted, or transmitted in any form or by any means, electronic, mechanical, photocopying, micro-filming recording or otherwise, or translated in any language, without the prior written permission of the copyright owner and the publisher. The book is sold subject to the condition that it shall not, by way of trade or otherwise, be lent, resold, hired out, or otherwise circulated without the prior publisher written consent in any form of binding or cover other than that in which it is published.

The views and opinions expressed in this book are author(s) own and the facts reported by him/her have been verified to the expert possible, and the publishers are not in any way liable for the same.

ISBN 13-978-81-8069-503-2 **ISBN 10-81-8069-503-4**

First Published 2009

Published and Printed by

Concept
Since 1974

Concept Publishing Company
Regd. Office:
A/15-16, Commercial Block, Mohan Garden
New Delhi-110059 (India)
Phones : 25351460, 25351794, ***Fax*** : 091-11-25357109
Email : publishing@conceptpub.com,
website: www.conceptpub.com

Editorial Office:
H-13, Bali Nagar, New Delhi-110 015, India.

Cataloging in Publication Data--*Courtesy:* D.K. Agencies (P) Ltd. <docinfo@dkagencies.com>

Palanithurai, G. (Ganapathy), 1953-
Rajiv Gandhi's vision on local governance / G. Palanithurai.
p. cm.
Includes index.
ISBN 13: 9788180695032 ISBN 10: 8180695034

1. Gandhi, Rajiv, 1944-1991--Political and social views. 2. Panchayat India. 3. Local government--India. 4. Democracy--India. 5. India-- Politics and government--1977- I. Title.

DDC 320.80954 22

Foreword

It was at the release of the Hindi version of my little book "Remembering Rajiv" on 21 August 2008 that his son, Rahul Gandhi, recalled his asking his father one weary morning at crack of dawn in the gruelling 1989 election campaign why he (his father) did not just give up all this and return to his first love, being a pilot? Rahul said his father replied that he just could not go back now because his Prime Ministership had taught him to "believe in the people of India". Rahul added that it was this "belief in the people" that was what shaped Rajivji's conviction that the key to good governance in our country lay in self-governance by the people themselves through Panchayati Raj in their respective habitats and communities.

As one who had been associated closely with Prime Minister Rajiv Gandhi from the beginning to the tragic end in his passion for Panchayati Raj, I was struck by the deep perception of this comment. It was precisely because Shri Rajiv Gandhi was deeply convinced that the people of India, rather than bureaucracy of India or the upper-echelon politicians of India, could best manage the affairs of the village that he found the answer to his quest for "Responsive Administration" in giving Constitutional status to the Institutions of Panchayati Raj. In his very first speech as Prime Minister after being elected in December 1984 by the highest majority ever attained, Prime Minister Rajiv Gandhi set the tone for his administration by stressing the need for "Responsive Administration". Later, he was to incorporate this as the twentieth point of the Revised 20-Point Programme announced from the ramparts of the Red Fort on Independence Day, 1986. To begin with, Rajivji thought responsive administration might be attained by managerial improvements in our system of administration, drawing particular inspiration from one young District Magistrate's experiment in the "Single Window" system of receiving and responding to petitions from the general public as well as setting aside one day in the week as "Grievance Redressal Day" rather in the manner of the Mughal Emperors' *Darbar-e-Aam*.

But by September 1986, when he addressed the All India Panchayat Parishad, it became increasingly clear that the Prime Minister was not searching for a managerial solution but a systemic solution. This he found in the concept of Panchyati Raj, advocated by Mahatma Gandhi as the very foundation of the Constitution of free India and later adopted by Pandit Jawaharlal Nehru with missionary zeal after reading the Report of the Balwantrai Mehta Study Group (1957). Rajivji asked himself why it was that with democracy flourishing in Parliament and the State Legislatures, India had become the world's largest democracy but remained the world's least representative democracy owing to every Panchayati Raj initiative from Gandhiji to Panditji having withered on the vine. He found answer to this conundrum in the fact that while the Constitution had made detailed provision for democracy at the Centre and the State Legislatures, there was no comparable provision for local self-government at the grassroots. At his initiative, Parliament eventually passed the longest and most detailed amendments ever made to the Constitution incorporating in Part IX detailed provisions for "The Panchayats" and in Part IXA for "The Municipalities".

I would not wish to quote from or paraphrase the rationale behind this most long-lasting contribution of Shri Rajiv Gandhi to the evolution of democracy in India because that will emerge from the pages that follow. What here I would like to do is to recall two private conversations which I had with him which put in perspective his more formal speeches on the subject.

One day he remarked to me that the biggest danger facing our country was "these young men in tight pants". I was a bit startled at this observation and enquired what he meant. He patiently explained that up until his mother's time, the large crowds of the poor and the deprived who would throng 1, Akbar Road every morning to meet her were content with her receiving their petitions and giving them a sympathetic hearing for a minute or two: *Sunwai* as it is called in Hindi. Things, however, were changing. The sons of these petitioners, now educated (or half-educated) in schools and mofussil colleges with poor facilities were abandoning the *dhotis* worn by their fathers, donning tight trousers as was the fashion in the Eighties, and spending all their waking hours abusing and criticizing the Government while waiting in every election to kick out the incumbent Government as a way of ventilating their frustrations. The fault, said Rajivji, lay not in these young men but in us, the governing elite, who had taught this generation that everything they receive was a boon from the *Mai Baap Sarkar*, that is, a government that behaves like parents towards an infant child. Since Government was incapable of meeting all the demands of this very demanding child, the danger lay in these young people eventually getting fed up with merely changing governments through the democratic process and resorting instead to violence and insurrection. The only way, said Rajivji, of preserving our democracy would be to replace the *Mai Baap Sarkar* with local self-government so that these very young persons would become responsible for the growth, development and welfare of their respective communities instead of merely performing the role of a sounding board for local grievances.

The second conversation I recall arose out of my asking him how long he thought it would take us to bring Panchayati Raj to complete efflorescence. "25 years!" he remarked. Startled and completely taken aback, I asked him why he thought it would take so long even after the Constitution is amended to secure full Panchayati Raj in letter and spirit. The conversation took place in October 1989, the month in which the Berlin Wall came tumbling down. Tangentially referring to that historic moment, Rajivji smiled and said that it had taken a mere seven decades for the Soviet Revolution which was accomplished in "Ten Days that Shook the World" to be brought to an end; if Panchayati Raj were to last forever, it should not be a Ten Day Revolution but a thorough systemic change in governance unfolding over an entire generation so that it fully takes root as the very foundation of our enduring democracy.

Fifteen years after the entry into force of the 73rd Constitutional Amendment, incorporated as Part IX of the Constitution, Panchayati Raj, as foreseen by Rajiv Gandhi, has indeed been made ineluctable, irreversible and irremovable. However, the Institutions of Panchayati Raj are still to be empowered with the effective devolution of Functions, Finances and Functionaries. Although some progress in this direction has been made in all States, and considerable progress has been made in some States, looking at the processes of devolution from an all-India perspective, it is clear that much still remains to be done to ensure, as Article 243G enjoins, that Panchayati Raj Institutions perform their duties as "institutions of local self-government". Rajivji's prophecy gives us yet one more decade to convert institutionalized Panchayati Raj into effective Panchayati Raj. I think that goal could be entirely attained within the lifetime of the next Government provided that Government is dedicated to the cause of "Inclusive Growth through Inclusive Governance".

If that were to happen, perhaps when I meet up with Rajivji again up there, I could tell him that we have accomplished in a year or two or less than he imagined the goal of full-scope, throughgoing Panchayati Raj. If we succeed, our country, our democracy and future generations to come are all safe. If, God forbid, we were to fail, then it will be endangering the indefinite continuance of the greatest achievement of independent India: translating Independence for the country into Freedom for her People. Succeed we can. Succeed we must.

New Delhi **Mani Shankar Aiyar**
31 October 2008

PS: Incidentally this Foreword is written on the 24th anniversary of Rajiv Gandhi being sworn in as Prime Minister of India in the immediate aftermath of the martyrdom of his mother.

Preface

Long back I was in a meeting with Shri L.C. Jain in Nagpur for a Panchayat leaders meet. Some of the volunteers distributed the speeches of some dignitaries on Panchayati Raj System. Shri L.C. Jain asked me "where is the speech of Rajiv Gandhi on Panchayati Raj?" I said right now I do not have the copy. But we can get it. He asked me to get it. I requested Mr. Mani Shankar Aiyar who was also on the dias to get a copy from Rajiv Gandhi Foundation. He got a copy of the speech and took photo copies and distributed among the participants. While delivering the speech L.C. Jain made it clear that the speeches of Rajiv Gandhi would give clarity to many of the issues which we discuss in many fora.

Whenever Mani Shankar Aiyar spoke about the New Panchayati Raj System he profusely quoted Rajiv Gandhi as to how he visualised a new system of governance at the grassroots. Subsequently, the Task Force in Rajiv Gandhi Foundation prepared a Charter of Panchayats to serve as article of faith which is based on the vision of Rajiv Gandhi and the general reality in the field. After reading some of the research articles and speeches of some of the prominent leaders, I thought that the speeches of Rajiv Gandhi should be brought to light for understanding the basic spirit behind democratic decentralization of powers in India.

Wherever I went I used to refer to the speeches of Rajiv Gandhi. Whenever I wrote article I quote profusely the speeches of Rajiv Gandhi. Based on the writings and speeches, demand for the speeches of Rajiv Gandhi has increased. Rajiv Gandhi introduced the 64th and 65th Amendments to the Constitution of India after a lengthy process of consultations with various stakeholders. Hence the spirit for decentralization of powers emanates from the efforts of Rajiv Gandhi. Hence it was increasingly felt that everyone should refer to the speeches of Rajiv Gandhi.

The speeches of Rajiv Gandhi had been already published in a multi-volume set and they are taken out and published in this work. I profusely acknowledge the painful works done by a team to edit the speeches and translate the same from Hindi to English and published by the Publication Division of the Ministry of Information and Broadcasting, Government of India.

I register my gratitude to Shri L.C. Jain who gave me clarity on many issues on Panchayati Raj in the initial stages and he spoke to me many times that Rajiv Gandhi's speeches on Panchayati Raj have to be circulated among the activists involved in Panchayati Raj activities which prompted me to bring out this work.

I express my profound thanks to Mr. Mani Shankar Aiyar for having brought to light the essence of the speeches of Rajiv Gandhi in all his speeches which again motivated me to undertake this small exercise.

I profusely express my thanks to Concept Publishing Company which is emerging as a specialist in bringing out a large number of books on New Panchayati Raj System in India.

I express my deep sense of gratitude to my colleagues working in the Department and the project with a sense of commitment and dedication for their valuable support extended to me for all my activities both academic and outreach. Last not the least, my family unit, my wife Ms. Mala, my kids Senthilvadivu and Aurobindh who always play a supportive role by not disturbing me and do their activities on their own.

G. Palanithurai

Contents

Contents

1

Introduction

The 73rd and 74th Amendments to the Constitution of India are the landmark events to break the barriers in the process of social and economic transformation of hitherto excluded and marginalized. The two historic amendments have got full potentials to transform the landscape of polity, society and economy at the grassroots. Both are equipped to empower the disempowered and disempower the dominant groups from domination over the marginalized and deprived. What is required is the marginalized and the deprived who are going to acquire power should be in a position to make use of the potentials. Those who fervently argue that the governments have to work for the poor, marginalized, underprivileged, and discriminated should facilitate the above groups to make use of the opportunity. It is a matter of power, position, decision-making, resource allocation, service delivery, governance and administration, which cannot be given to the weak or marginalized automatically even though it is mandated. Powers should flow from the dominant to the marginalized and from bureaucrats to the elected representatives at the grassroots. One cannot assume power will flow automatically.

In general, people want to find solution to the existing stagnation in the process of devolution of powers administratively or managerially. As a student of Political Science and as a person hailing from obscurity, I know the struggle of the poor in India and how they have to struggle to claim their rightful dues even when they are guaranteed by the Constitution. It is always a tussle between the provisions of the

Constitution and the practices and procedures of the communities. Constitution grants a lot of things to the voiceless but the community denies all those benefits wherever the poor, deprived and marginalized are weak and powerless. It is a country known for unevenness, disparities and discriminations on many fronts. In our six decades of experience in democracy and development we have seen the transformations only in a few segments of the society. Though democracy provides scope for all segments of the people to solve their problems and achieve development through representative institutions, people could not raise their voice and even if they raise their voice they are not heard and even if they are heard, they are not respected and responded. The voiceless people are coerced to exercise their right to vote through mediation by the local bigwigs belonging to the dominant class and communities.

Many of the fine provisions of the Constitution of India are inoperative and ineffective as they are not claimed rightfully and intensively by the stakeholders. It is obvious from our experience that those who lose their power and privileges by the provisions of the Constitution are knowledgeable about the full implications of the provisions of new laws. But the people who are going to gain power and advantage of those provisions are neither aware nor are in a position to assert their rights as they are weak and powerless socially and economically. The political equality the deprived has got through the Constitution has not altered the social and economic conditions. The strong presence of feudal mindset, caste structure, and patriarchy destabilized many of the efforts of the governments.

For effective decentralization of powers to grassroots institutions, a strong political will is an imperative on the part of the state leadership, Secondly it requires a fine legislation by incorporating the spirit of the 73rd and 74th Amendments to the Constitution of India. To translate the provisions of the Act into action, a committed bureaucracy is needed. The existing bureaucracy which is antithetical to devolution and hence the mindset of the bureaucracy has to be changed. To get full implications of devolution, the skill, capacity and capability of the elected representatives have to be enhanced. Last not the least people have to be mobilized to participate in democratization of society and in the process of development. In Indian context devolution means devolving powers from the State Government to local bodies. The State Governments which have got perspective in people's democracy and participatory development will take up steps on their own for devolution of powers. Others need centralised drive. Hence for proper devolution of powers, initiatives have to be taken from the Central Government and from the society by mobilizing the people to get their powers on their own.

Against this background, one has to look at the 73rd and 74th Amendments to the Constitution of India. These two amendments have enough potentials to alter the nature of governance and power relations among the unequals at the grassroots. It has got tremendous potentials to solve the problem of exclusion. It is unfortunate that these potentials are not known to the people who are expected to gain power. People who are in power and who are going to lose power have understood thoroughly the full implications of the two amendments. Having understood the implications, they have devised mechanism suitably to keep the power with them through new strategies. Wife or daughter is being sponsored for local body elections when the seat is reserved for women and farm labourer or maid servant is being sponsored by the landlord or the dominant leader if the seat is reserved for *Dalits*.

Even after fourteen years of the enactment of the amendments to the Constitution, people are not aware of the full implications of the amendments. Lot of confusions are created in the process of implementing the amendments in letter and spirit. Sometimes confusions are created deliberately with an objective of delaying the process. One major confusion is created by posing the question whether the Panchayat is a state subject or not. Some are arguing that it is a state subject, the centre cannot do anything for or against the state in the process of implementation. Officials in the Central Government and State Governments, legal exponents, NGOs and activists are giving varying views for the same amendments. L.C. Jain an exponent on this subject headed many committees and a person with eminence and erudition gave a logical argument that after passing the 73rd Amendment that there is no reason to proclaim Panchayati Raj as a state subject and hence it is under the mercy of the State Government.

The 73rd and 74th Amendments are the outcome of the failure of the states in making the local bodies as institutions of self-governance. The two Amendments have gone through a process and two-third members of the National Parliament have approved and more than 50 per cent of the State Governments have accepted this new dispensation. In essence, it is a new governance structure and it has its own legitimacy for governance. Even after bringing the Panchayat in Part IX of the Constitution if we bring the same old argument of classifying the Panchayat as a subject as a state subject and hence the fate of the local bodies will be determined by the State Government and there is no logical solution to this issue. It is a kind of escapism, whether it has been argued either by the State Government or by the Central Government. A new interpretation has to be given constitutionally to protect the legitimacy of the Panchayats, and necessary remedial measures should be taken.

For any issue to be clarified a framework is necessary. For democratic decentralization of powers in the new context, basic framework was evolved by Rajiv Gandhi. He was instrumental in bringing constitutional amendments to make the grassroots institutions as institutions of self-governance. Though he failed to succeed in his attempt, he had done the base work which is solid and referral. Thus in Indian context, the framework developed by Rajiv Gandhi is fundamental. The framework developed by Rajiv Gandhi may be used to give clarity to these issues for creating a New System of Local Governance in India. The speeches delivered by Rajiv Gandhi in Parliament and in various conventions and workshops are historic and they are passing for classic which have to be considered as the basic framework for decentralization of power in India. It is unfortunate that the framework has been forgotten. Many of those who speak on local governance in India have not gone through the speeches of Late Rajiv Gandhi which are so important as the new conceptualization has gone through a process of series of discussions and deliberations he held with various stakeholders to address the issues of democracy and development at grassroots.

If the full text of the speeches of Rajiv Gandhi relating to the framework is read no one will raise any question on it. If they are understood no one will seek administrative solution to the issues of the Panchayati Raj System. The present devolution process is totally a centralized drive. When it is a centralized drive without having any clear understanding at the ground, it will run into trouble and to overcome the trouble the demand for devolution has to come from the below. Thus it is a process of accent and decent. This requires a massive and intensive movement at the grassroots. A movement has to emerge from the grassroots for proper devolution of powers. All those who are working in the Panchayats are working in project-and-event mode but not in developing a mass movement. Organisations and institutions have done enough work to generate documents. At the ground level, the conditions are not positive. Whatever excellence we have witnessed in grassroots is inadequate. They could not form a critical mass to bring change. People who are spearheading macro and micro movements for socio-economic transformation have to see the potentials of the new dispensation. A large number of organisations working at different levels for the *Dalits*, minorities, women, *Adivasis* and other marginalized should make use of the Panchayats for the emancipation of the above groups. The civil society organisations which are working for empowerment of the people and weaker sections should make use of the new dispensation. Strengthening of grassroots institutions will strengthen the base of democracy and deepen the value of democracy. But in reality at present everyone is looking for another Mahatma to mobilize people. Even the Gandhians have failed to understand the significance of the new dispensation. The need of the hour is a mass movement from below not a sporadic attempt in the form of project events. To mobilize the mass for social and political action one has to create awareness among the people about the positive implications of the two constitutional amendments.

There is yet another serious issue which has its own implication in grassroots governance. It is the issue arising out of 'Globalization'. Grassroots leaders are not aware of the implications of the process of globalization, and the Panchayats are victims to the globalization process. On water mining, sand mining and on many other issues, Panchayats are not able to do anything. There are instances where some of the NGOs raising voices against globalization yet the victimization activities are going on. If Panchayat representatives have sufficient knowledge about globalization, they will take steps to avoid threats if any, and at the same time, they will make use of the opportunity, if any from globalization. Who is competent to do this? It is imperative that a training module has to be prepared and training has to be conducted. It should be on globalization and natural resource management at the grassroots level.

It is a trend throughout the world that people oppose globalization openly and vociferously yet globalization process is on vigorously and speedily. For decentralization of powers everywhere we find open support but devolution does not work as vigorously as globalization. Globalization works for the rich and decentralization works for the poor and hence the mechanisms are in two different modes. Unless a mass movement is developed for decentralization, effective decentralization of power is not possible. It is almost a civil struggle or another struggle for independence of the oppressed and the poor.

It is reported that 170 districts in India are "disturbed districts" and virtually they are not under the effective administration of the Indian state. Almost one-third of our country is not with us. No one is looking at it from the perspective of devolution of powers. Unless people are engaged and involved in development activities with powers and responsibilities, the youth will seek alternative employment through the extremist organisations. In a populous country engaging people is an imperative need. In our country, our political parties are engaging them for their political activities.

It has been argued from the beginning in Tamil Nadu that devolution of powers to Panchayats will be real, effective and meaningful only when powers devolve from the Central Government to the State Government. It is argued that the powers enjoyed by the State Governments are equal to the powers enjoyed by the local bodies in the western countries. It is proposed that the existing framework of power devolution will weaken the State Governments. Against this background the State Governments should look at the devolution of powers. Pressure has to be exerted to the Central Government to devolve powers to the State Governments. This is an argument of the State Government. It is to be debated.

It has been noticed that the civil society organisations are working in a few districts, a few blocks, a few states, on *Dalit* issue, women issue and children issues through the Panchayati Raj. They are yet to start the movement activities for devolution of powers. Civil society organisations are still in project mode. Even Gandhian institutions and Gandhians have not played their due role in mobilizing the people for establishing 'Gram Rajyam'. They have missed a lot of opportunities. The emerging Panchayati Raj Institutions and Self-Help Groups can be effectively used to empower the people. A mass movement can be easily mobilized through the new dispensation.

In every village the customary Panchayat works effectively and vigorously. It has its own resource base. The natural resource management is with the Panchayat. They manage effectively by the natural resources. In some of the places the customary Panchayat is dominated by the caste Hindus excluding the *Dalits* and women. In a few places the same includes both *Dalits* and women. In some parts, they collude with the constitutional Panchayats. Unless a formal channel is created between the customary Panchayats and constitutional Panchayats for synergy, the customary Panchayats will take over the activities of the constitutional Panchayats headed by *Dalits* and women.

Despite all the drawbacks, the Panchayats have started transforming the living conditions of the poor. Arguments are projected based on the experience of the people throughout the world that decentralization will work effectively if:

(a) There is a strong presence of a middle class;
(b) Land reform is done;
(c) Larger presence of civil society organisations is ensured;
(d) High literacy rate; and
(e) Adequate powers and finances are with grassroots institutions.

In India a new proposition is emerging. Wherever committed leadership with a vision and capability is emerging, there decentralization works effectively. India is contributing to the emergence of a new theory. In India a large number of leaders are emerging as models by their excellent performance through which they have changed the gloomy scenario at the grassroots. The six-decade activities of the State and Central Governments have been surpassed by the activities of the new institutions under the new leadership.

It is a paradox in India that we have a Ministry of Panchayati Raj in Government of India and now it is a deriving force to shape governance to grassroots in rural areas. What happened to the urban local bodies? Is there any ministry looking into the governance matter seriously? Urban Development Ministry is seriously concentrating on projects rather than governance issues. At least in the rural areas, in the absence of Panchayati Raj, one would find community governance arrangement. But in the urban areas we find only individuals not communities. Governance arrangement is an imperative need for the urban areas. But the Ministry is not doing anything in this regard. It is always logical to look at local governance integrally both for rural and urban community not in isolation. But unfortunately nobody talks about the urban governance.

It is unfortunate that in India, media is not sensitized on this issue of decentralization. A new transformative leadership is emerging but the idea has not disseminated. In Tamil Nadu an experiment was conducted with media which brought tremendous results. With the support of a popular vernacular daily "*Dinamalar*" the Rajiv Gandhi Chair for Panchayati Raj Studies, Department of Political Science and Development Administration, Gandhigram Rural University, has brought out one-full page material on Panchayati Raj entitled "Panchayat Malar" for 54 weeks with the support of The Hunger Project. At present the media involvement is very less. As the media involved in the freedom struggle, it has to engage itself in decentralization also.

Capacity building is yet another major step in this direction. In the absence of capacity building policy, the capacity building exercises are taken up by different agencies with different perspectives. But the coverage is not even one-third of leaders. The training institutions barring a few are the places for punishment for officials. Unwanted officials are put in the training institutions. From this scenario one would find the level of the commitment and capability of the trainers working in training institutions. Of course, there are exceptions and models such as Anita Kaul. Training is to be conducted massively and support structure has to be created to support leaders who are struggling in the field.

The newly-recruited representatives for local governance need capacity building which is so serious and imperative. But unfortunately we do not have any policy for capacity building at national level or at regional level barring a few states. It is our general attitude that politicians do not require training. Our MLAs, MPs and ministers have no formal training. In the same way representatives of the local bodies do not require training. This is the general view. Unless they are trained properly and perspectively chaos will be in local governance. A large number of representatives are drawn from the poor strata of the society who require proper orientation and capacity building.

At the ground, every Gram Panchayat should have administrative unit not only to administer development but also to manage data. At present all confusions in administration, allocation and management are due to the absence of data base at grassroots. Only at the district level we have the data base and down below the district there is no strong scientific data base. Even after establishing governing units, if there is no data base how are we going to plan? Hence data base has to be created in each Gram Panchayat, each Block Panchayat, and each District Panchayat.

Yet another issue is planning from below. Still it is in theory excepting in Kerala. There are sporadic experiments in many states. Panchayats can at least prepare a wish list and ask the Government Departments to work on their list. This kind of pressure alone will alter the existing scenario of working on supply and not on demand.

In India the local bodies are confronting a very serious problem. Even after the departure of the British, though we proclaim ourselves as representative democracy, the democratic elements have not taken deep roots as a culture. Our democracy is always equated with election. Election is one of the aspects in democracy. Even this election is seen only for the National Parliament and State Legislature. Elections should form part of all organisations and institutions which are governed democratically. Our country is full of rulers in the name of leaders. Actually they do not have the mass support but they are ruling the mass. This ruler-culture has to be changed and hence the grassroots leaders should not follow the model of our regional and national leaders and they have to set an example and they should not become rulers. They should really be the leaders and they are the models for the regional and national leaders. Hence, many leadership schools have to be created to train the Panchayat leaders. The training institutions are leadership schools. By doing so, little republics can be created otherwise our Panchayat system will enable the leaders to create their own kingdoms.

To alter the existing scenario a mass movement has to be created from the grassroots. At this juncture, an individual's role has to be appreciated. Mani Shankar Iyer now is playing the role of S.K. Dey.

A lot of efforts have been taken by the UPA Government in strengthening Panchayati Raj. It is to be noted here that a Joint Parliamentary Committee which was constituted by the NDA Government made a thorough analysis of the status of devolution of powers. It indicted both the Central and State Governments for its negligence in taking earnest efforts to devolve powers. The Committee criticized both the Central and State Governments for their lapses. Yet, there was no action. But, after the formation of the UPA Government, a new Ministry was created for Panchayati Raj and its creation has made a point known to all that a new mechanism has been devised to monitor the whole process of decentralization of powers. A Minister was appointed but there was no team. But now it has been created by the Minister by selecting officials sensitive on devolution of powers. It is also known in Indian polity that the Panchayati Raj Minister never gets recognition. Even from the days of S.K. Dey, it is history that the Panchayati Raj Minister and the Ministry had to suffer as they always work with the people and for the people. Working in this Ministry, the Minister and the officials have to face difficult situations. The Finance Minister who speaks about globalization will get appreciation but the Minister who speaks about decentralization will get brick-bats even though the outward support for decentralization by the public is strong.

By the earnest efforts of the Panchayati Raj Ministry as a follow-up to the Round Table Resolutions, several steps have been taken. In the resolutions of the Round Table the following points have been reiterated:

1. Panchayats are not implementing agencies,
2. They are institutions of self-government,
3. Power should be given through law,
4. While distributing activities among the three-tiers there should not be any overlapping,
5. Law of subsidiary has to be maintained,
6. Functionaries have to be fixed corresponding to functions,

7. A Panchayati Raj administrative and technical service cadre has to be created,
8. Merger of DRDA with District Panchayats and change of nomenclature,
9. Finance on the pattern of activity mapping,
10. Financial allocation for Panchayati Raj in State and Central budgets,
11. Larger amount as untied fund for Panchayats,
12. Untied grants to Panchayats from Planning Commission,
13. Gram Sabha has to be strengthened,
14. Ward Sabha can be created,
15. Enabling conditions should be created to ensure women and *Dalit* participation,
16. Constitution of District Planning Committee is mandatory,
17. Planning exercise has to start from the Panchayat,
18. A women-and-*Dalit* component plan could be created,
19. Creation of parallel bodies has to be totally avoided,
20. A strong tie-up between Panchayats and SHGs,
21. Laws contradictory to the 73rd Amendment should be made null and void,
22. Assessment has to be made every year by using Devolution Index,
23. Annual Report on devolution has to be prepared,
24. All complicated issues in elections have to be sorted out by strengthening the Election Commission,
25. Adequate attention has to be given to capacity building,
26. Establishing e-governance at grassroots, and
27. A vibrant accountability has to be established.

The Round Table prevailed upon the Planning Commission that the 12th Finance Commission allocation should be sent to the three-tier Panchayats through the State Government by following the principle of fiscal federalism as per the roles assigned to each tier. The amount transferred to the State Government has to be transferred to the Panchayats within fifteen days failing which the State Government has to pay the interest also to the Panchayats. To transfer funds, Panchayati institutions of all the three tiers should be in position. Otherwise the State cannot get the allocated money.

Devolution of powers has been resisted by various forces of which the parallel bodies are the major obstacle. The parallel bodies have been designed by the Central Government departments through their schemes and by donor agencies through their projects. The Central Government has created a powerful parallel body called the MPLAD scheme. The State Governments have also followed the same to thwart decentralization by introducing the MLA Constituency Development Fund. The MPLAD has been reviewed and unequivocally and it has been stated that it is a colossal waste of money and that the money is misused. Hence the National Advisory Committee has recommended the scheme to be abolished. Once it is done away with the MLA Constituency Development Fund will also be done away with misuse of money. It has not only recommended the above but also recommended 27 Action Points to the governments. They are:

A. Recommendations for Implementation by the Government of India (GOI)

(i) The additional allocations recommended by the Central Finance Commission to States (and, in particular, the supplementary sources to local governments) should be contingent upon the States fully implementing the suggestions offered by the GOI and also the recommendations of the State Finance Commissions in relation to LSGIs.

(ii) A Devolution Index needs to be prepared for all States and at least one-third of the allocation of the Centrally sponsored schemes in the Panchayat functional domain or block grants (when introduced) may be allocated to State Governments on the basis of this Index. The Devolution Index may be prepared by the States based on a framework developed by the GOI.

(iii) PRIs should be the principal agency (instead of District Collectors) for schemes such as MPLADS. The MPLADS funds may be deposited with Zila Parishads as untied funds and Members of Parliament may indicate their preferences for schemes/programmes to the concerned Zila Parishad or Block Panchayats/ Gram Panchayats, which should be implemented by the Panchayats as part of the overall village/area/ district plan.

(iv) Several new schemes, missions and projects such as education mission, health mission, employment guarantee scheme, mid-day meal scheme and universalisation of ICDS programmes are being handled by the Union Government in pursuance of the National Common Minimum Programme. Local self-government institutions should own, manage, monitor and control these new programmes and missions.

(v) Given the Union Government's considerable influence in dealing with States, this can be leveraged to promote State devolution to local governments. The bilateral and multilateral funding agencies may be advised that their support for projects related to the functional domain of local governments as envisaged in the Eleventh and the Twelfth Schedules has to be contingent upon implementation through elected local governments.

(vi) Articles 243N and 243ZF stipulate that all laws inconsistent with Part IX of the Constitution shall lapse upon the expiration of one year from the date on which the 73rd and 74th Amendments came into effect. The Union Government can constitute a task force to identify all such inconsistencies in Union laws as well as in the laws in each State for preparing a report within three months. Such inconsistent provisions of the law will be deemed to have been repealed, failing which the Union can direct States to ensure conformity with the Constitution and citizens could invoke the writ jurisdiction of the higher judiciary.

(vii) The Eleventh and Twelfth Schedules listed 29 and 18 subjects, which come within the purview of the local governments. While the principle of subsidiary should guide allocation of subjects, the economies of scale, managerial capacity and applicability of services across several Panchayats and other factors will determine a rational division of functions. Such a division will also be State- specific, given the diverse historical experiences and different levels/types of evolution of local government tiers. A task force should undertake this activity—mapping to be implemented by States. All future allocations and assignment of responsibilities should be based on such distribution of functions.

(viii) The fiscal responsibility and accountability of local governments are the cause of much concern. The Union Government may consider enacting legislation incorporating mandatory measures to promote fiscal prudence and accountability in local governments across the country. Such legislation should also include provisions defining the responsibilities of State and Union Governments in respect of funds flow and personnel matters, so that fairness, predictability and transparency will be institutionalized. The law should encompass non-partisan and fair procedures.

(ix) A national 'IT for Panchayati Raj' programme should be launched immediately with the following three initiatives:

(a) A nationally networked and computerized system, including the treasury system, is a necessary prerequisite to effectively monitor fund flows and utilization and to facilitate devolution. The Union Government will need to launch a fund for this purpose and operationalise the national computerized network within one year.

(b) A series of information outlets like STD/PCO booths for disseminating information and making available various forms, services and transactions to the public can be set-up by encouraging local entrepreneurs. A combination of services for the consumption of both the government and the public through these units will make them commercially viable and socially relevant.

(c) Back-end support by parallel ICT efforts for computerization of various services can become operational with networking across Gram Panchayats, Taluka Panchayats, Zila Panchayats and Panchayat departments at the state headquarters.

(x) The concept of district plans/district budgeting should be introduced during the year 2006-07. This should be based on block grants to districts. The basic planning exercise should be undertaken at the Gram Panchayat level. The use of spearhead teams or project facilitation teams should be ensured. The project facilitation teams should be given intensive training through the district capacity building organisation set up with a multidisciplinary background as part of the Zila Parishad. The exercise of district planning and district budgeting could be linked to the backward district fund suggested by the Planning Commission but should not be limited to the backward district fund.

(xi) MPs and MLAs ought to periodically declare specific details of the works done under the MPLADS and MLA Fund schemes. Similarly, in Parliament, it is suggested that such details may be shared (with a full discussion with questions raised), which the concerned member may be required to defend.

B. Recommendations for Implementation by State Governments

(i) Concerted efforts towards better accountability and performance of the local bureaucracy need to be pursued. For this purpose, the provisions of the revised Right to Information Bill need to be invoked and implemented particularly with the help of PRIs and other agencies.

(ii) It is necessary to reconsider the current funding system, with added-emphasis being placed on Panchayats generating more internal revenues at all the three levels with matching government funds. External funds with no commitment to raise internal resources could make the PRIs irresponsible/corrupt.

(iii) The States have to increase the share of transfers to PRIs from State Governments as untied grants by (a) consolidating State schemes with broad rural development objectives into united grants as Kerala has done; (b) making these grants a share of State revenues; (c) explicitly defining (through state legislation) formulae to allocate grant to Panchayati Raj Institutions; and (d) transferring collection of village taxes, such as land revenue and irrigation tax, to PRIs. The formula of transfer should not only give weightage to population and poverty but also to efficiency in increasing the sources of revenues of PRIs through own and assigned taxes and increasing their capacity to collect.

(iv) The focus of decentralization should rest on outcome-orientedness rather than just measuring the inputs and evaluating the utilization and percentages thereof. For each tier of LSGI, a Panchayat-metric grid may be evolved, which will become an evaluation framework for any LSGI.

(v) The quality of work done by Panchayats should be closely monitored by teams of media persons, civil society members, such Panchayat leaders from the neighbouring districts. The Panchayats should be graded and future funds linked to this grading. Strengthening financial management and audit procedures will also enhance the accountability of local bodies, to their Standing Committees and people's representatives as well to the government.

(vi) Consultations may be held with State Governments to enact and implement PESA uniformly across all the nine States in conformity with the Central Act, with the requisite IEC activities in order to create greater awareness and understanding.

(vii) In the structure of Gram Panchayats, Taluka Panchayats and Zila Panchayats, there is a disconnection between the Gram Panchayat President and Taluka Panchayat. There ought to be a system of representation of Gram Panchayat Presidents in the Taluka Panchayat with direct election of the Taluka Panchayat President. A similar system ought to be in place for Zila Panchayats as well.

(viii) *Women empowerment:* States may take up measures such as the provision of women-component plans in the budgets of PRIs, linkages with Self-Help Groups (SHGs), encouragement to political parties to put up women candidates and opportunity to women to serve a full term (when they are elected to posts in the Panchayati Raj System), Mahila Sabhas (or equivalent) to facilitate women's concerns and priorities being raised in meetings of Gram Sabhas and Ward Sabhas (or equivalent sub-Gram Sabha forums) and fix quorum for womens' participation in Gram Sabhas and Ward sub-Gram Sabha fora.

(ix) The State Governments should put in place and implement a comprehensive training and capacity building programme for elected representatives of local self-government institutions and Panchayati Raj Institutions. Such training programmes should preferably be completed with universal coverage within one year of the holding of elections to these bodies. The Central Government should facilitate and incentivise such programmes through monetary and other support. External expertise should be sought liberally for carrying out these training programmes.

(x) States could afford the option of doing away with one of the Panchayat levels after the implications of efficiency, equity and participation have been studied.

(xi) Institutional links between political decentralization (in the form of PRIs) and administrative decentralization (in the form of user committees) promoted by external donor projects need to be strengthened.

(xii) Panchayats are often too large: the Kerala Panchayats cover about 23,000 people and the Orissa and West Bengal Panchayats some 15 to 20 villages. Smaller bodies need to be formed for operational purposes. It is suggested that for each function of the Gram Panchayat, the Gram Sabha be a forum where people can volunteer or be selected to be part of the Committee looking after a specific function, e.g. MDM, PDS, FFW, health, Anganwadi, lights, water etc. A member of the Gram Panchayat can be identified for each of these Committees for good-quality service delivery leading to development and excellence.

C. Recommendations that will Require Legislative Action

(i) Electoral rolls for all elections—local, state and national—should be common. The Constitution provides for separate electoral rolls for local governments. The practice of adopting the Assembly electoral rolls with the Election Commission of India and State Election Commissions functioning in coordination could be universally adopted by consensus and appropriate incentives and assistance provided to facilitate such uniform procedures.

(ii) The State Finance Commission is appointed under Article 243I and its functions are similar to those envisaged under Article 280 for the Central Finance Commission. Making the two Commissions coterminous will require an amendment to Article 243I, facilitating the appointment of a State Finance Commission by the Governor at the expiry of every fifth year, or at such earlier times as the Governor considers necessary.

(iii) Article 243K may be amended to extend the power of reserving constituencies for various sections, and the power of delimitation of constituencies to State Election Commissions, to be exercised in consultation with the State Government.

(iv) The district tier of local government should represent both rural and urban populations. Article 243D needs to be amended facilitating election of a single representative body at the district level for the population, rural or urban. Correspondingly, Article 243ZD (providing for the Committee for District Planning) will become redundant.

Yet another drive at the Centre is that the Departments of the Central Government operating rural development schemes have been made to agree that those schemes have to be implemented through the Panchayats and not through any parallel body and this process has been monitored.

Further the Panchayati Raj Ministry has taken two issues for immediate monitoring: training and District Planning Committee. District Planning Committee activities have been monitored. Under the employment guarantee scheme 50 per cent of the works have to be given to Panchayats, to implement the resolutions and to monitor the activities, periodical meetings of the Ministers of the Panchayati Raj System of the State Governments has been fixed. One meeting was conducted in Kochin.

Before 2007, all Gram Panchayats should be given computer and the administration be computerized. The Ministry has taken earnest steps to conduct a dialogue with the World Bank on parallel body creation while giving grants to various development projects. In order to strengthen the hands of the Panchayati Raj Ministry, the National Advisory Council has made two sets of recommendations to the Central Government and State Governments.

In order to activate the planning process from below, for the Eleventh Plan period, Panchayati Raj Ministries of all the State Governments should meet and prepare a road map.

Mani Shankar Iyer is swimming against the currents. His initiatives of strengthening Panchayats will succeed only when there is a people's movement from below. Civil society organisations have to perform two immediate functions, namely, mobilizing the people for demanding more power to Panchayats and build the capacity of the local body leaders. Youth in every village have to be involved in this endeavour.

In many of the occasions, explanations and interpretations are given to the New Panchayati Raj System in India from varied perspectives and sometimes misleading interpretations are also given. To avoid this, speeches of Rajiv Gandhi are compiled here for the benefit of the readers. Since Rajiv Gandhi took initiative for constitutionalising Panchayats, his vision and understanding of Panchayats, have to be seen perspectively. Against this background the important speeches of Rajiv Gandhi on Panchayats are compiled.

2

Panchayat must be Development Oriented

When we think of development programmes two different approaches come to mind. One approach, which was current immediately after Independence was that large-scale projects should be taken up to modernise the country. It was assumed that with development, the benefits would automatically percolate down to the poorest of the villages. We took long strides in this direction and crores of people were raised above the poverty line. However, even though a larger number of people were benefited, the poorest of the poor, especially the *Harijans* and *Adivasis* were so backward, so oppressed and weak that they were unable to derive any benefits from the programmes. We, therefore, had to devise special programmes to improve the condition of these sections. Our effort was to reach the lowest strata of our people. The Twenty-Point Programme is an effort in this direction.

Another thing that strikes one in regard to developmental work is the attitude of certain sections. They want to do nothing themselves to ameliorate their own lot. They think that everything should be done for them. They see the government as the guardian who must distribute the goodies, while they themselves may sit at home and wait for the bonanza. When nothing comes their way, they move to stage *dharnas* and strikes. But they will not come out to do any constructive work. This is a most dangerous tendency and so long as it persists, the fruits of development will never reach the poorest of the country.

Development does not mean merely the development of cities such as Delhi, Kolkata or Mumbai. If it were only a question of developing a few cities there would be no difficulty. We would soon be able to compete with the United States or Japan. Development has to mean the development of our villages. It is the villages that must be transformed. Indeed, once the villages are developed the cities will be automatically benefited, for the pressure on the cities will be lifted, the unending migration from villages to cities will be checked. People, instead of fleeing from villages, will stay back and work in the villages, and as a result the villages will progress. We must, therefore, shed the mentality of depending on the Government for everything. This can best be achieved through Panchayati Raj. Your endeavour should be our endeavour.

The community must decide for itself what activity would be beneficial to it; what are the things that the Central Government must do, what the State Governments must do, what can be taken up at the district level, and most important, what are the things that the people must themselves do through the Panchayats. It is clear that until the Panchayats are activated they will continue to lack strength, notwithstanding all the conferences we may hold, all the speeches we may make here in the cities. Another thing is that if we continue to devise schemes from above, large sections of the population will be left high and dry, and the flow of benefits from development will pass over their heads like water on a duck's back, for it is not possible for the Government agencies to reach each and every individual and to guide him and tell him to do this or that. This task is for you, for the Panchayats to undertake. Till there is this involvement, full benefits of the developmental schemes will continue to elude us.

You must see to it that people are fully involved in developmental programmes. We must change this tendency of waiting for the Government to dig this drain or build that culvert. I will give you an example from my own constituency. During one of my tours I call upon a group of villagers waiting by the roadside. They stopped me and pointed to a minor canal obstructing the road. It was perhaps a metre across and half a metre deep. I saw that when more villagers came to join us they just walked across the canal. The villagers requested me to have a culvert built over the canal. I said, we would see what could be done. At the same time I pointed out that the work did not really require any large effort and that having the Government undertake it would be unduly time-consuming, what with the CPWD coming into it and inviting tenders and so on. All that was required was to place a couple of girders across the canal. I can give you hundreds of such instances. This is the kind of mentality which we have to change. So long as this mentality is not shed, so long as people do not involve themselves in the process of development, fruits of progress will not reach the people. In January 1948, soon after Independence, Gandhiji had said: "True democracy cannot be worked by twenty men sitting at the Centre; it has to be worked from below by the people of every village." Writing in *Young India* twenty years before that, he had said: "*Swaraj* is to be obtained by educating the masses to a sense of their capacity to regulate and control authority." And Panditji said: "It is not good enough to work for the people, the only way is to work with the people, and give them a sense of working for themselves; development work can be executed only if the people take the responsibility in their own hands."

Gandhiji and Panditji have thus taught us that unless we reach the poorest in the villages the roots of our democracy cannot be strengthened. As someone just pointed out, if we had followed what our intellectuals have to say in books and newspaper articles, our country would have broken up in the last thirty-five years. If our country is still strong and united, it is due to the strength of its people, the enthusiasm of its people. We have not been able to derive the fullest benefit from that strength, that enthusiasm because we have not made democracy reach the villages. It can be done through Panchayati Raj. That is why we are giving so much attention to it.

It is now many years since Panchayati Raj was introduced in the country with great fanfare. There was much enthusiasm among the people. But over the years the momentum has dissipated and the machine appears to have come to a halt. It needs rewinding. After all what is the source from which the power of the Panchayats is derived? If the Panchayats have to depend on the money provided by the State administration or the district administration, they can never gain any strength. If the panchayats do not stand on their own feet they can never make progress. And the panchayats will be able to stand on their own feet when they show the political will to find resources in the villages they cover. This is not to say that they must entirely depend on local resources, but so long as there is no involvement of the people, so long as there is no political will to organise local resources, the panchayats cannot become strong. We have seen this happens in various States. The State that flinches from the task of mobilising resources is not able to make any progress. I have just returned from a three-day tour of West Bengal. I saw how the Sixth Plan worked there. The State Government thought that rather than going to the people of the State for money it would be better to ask the Centre for it. The Centre paid out its share, which the State Government used. But they did not use their own share and consequently a third of the outlay for the Sixth Plan has not been utilised. Thirty-two per cent of the Plan funds for power generation were not invested, some 40 per cent of the funds under rural development and agriculture were not used. The same thing happened in the case of funds for irrigation and drinking water for the villages. And why? For the simple reason that the State Government did not have the political will to mobilise its own resources, and the failure to do so resulted in the work of development being stalled. They are now ruining it. If they had spent the money, there would have been more power generation today, more irrigation, more drinking water. Now they are blaming the Centre for not doing this, that and the other. The root of the trouble, of course, lay in the unwillingness to mobilise their share of the resources. This is where the panchayats come in. If the panchayats do not mobilise the resources of the villages, how can the villagers make any progress? What will happen if you want money for everything from the Centre? The whole administrative machinery will set itself up in the villages: there will be an office with a few clerks, a peon, a stenographer and what not and the money intended for development will be diverted to support the administrative paraphernalia.

We cannot do from above what can be done with speed and vigour at the grassroots. We cannot do the work that the Panchayats neglect to do, just as the Panchayats cannot do the work that we do. Your part of the work is as important as ours. Neither is less important than the other. If anything, the work that you are required to do is more fundamental, for the strength in our work, that of preserving the unity and integrity of the country and safeguarding its borders, is derived from your work. When we go to the villages we see a lot of enthusiasm, but the enthusiasm will last only so long as work is vigorously pursued. If you slacken, the enthusiasm will evaporate, there will be erosion of the country's strength and the enemies of the country, within or outside, will accelerate their efforts to weaken and destroy the country. Thus, if we want to see India strong and united, the work of the Panchayats is of paramount importance. Without it the country cannot make progress. You must voluntarily take upon yourself this responsibility. In a way, many of your responsibilities have been taken away from you. The work now entrusted to District Rural Development Agencies should have been under your charge. But since the Panchayats did not exist, and they did not exist because no elections were held, another agency had to be appointed to undertake the work. We have to reverse this process. If the trend continues, the Panchayati Raj movement will be gradually weakened. We must put it back on the rails and try to restrict the scope of various other agencies and departments that have been brought into being. These, of course, cannot be wound up right away, before the Panchayats are strong enough to take over their functions. But we have to try and reverse this trend. We will certainly extend to you all the help you need. All of us, the Central Government, the State Governments and you at the Panchayat level, must consider how best this is to be done. There are no ready answers. It will take time, it will raise a debate. We are ready for the debate and we are ready to devote time for this, but the suggestions and ideas have to come from you and from the Government, how best we can press the panchayats into the work of development. It has been our experience in many States that when the responsibility for formulating plans was assigned to Panchayats, no plans were formulated. The example of Uttar Pradesh readily comes to mind. We sanctioned a certain sum of money for road development in a district and told the people that they should themselves decide how the money was to be spent. It was a matter of some 200 kilometres of road. They sat down and debated the matter. When I again visited the area two or three months later and asked about the road they said they had reached the decision that each village should have 200 metres assigned to it. Now this is not the way to do things. Who is going to derive any benefit from the 200 metres of road? They should have grouped ten, fifteen or twenty villages and constructed a *pucca* road. And this is not so only in Uttar Pradesh. We have seen the same thing happening in other States too. Whenever the responsibility for a basic decision is assigned to the Panchayats, they try to look for the easiest solution, with the result that instead of a decision we have a non-decision and the work of development is stalled. If this is to be rectified, the quality of the panchayats must be improved. Some training and education will be needed. It is for you to consider how best this is to be achieved. But without this you cannot expect to be entrusted with the responsibility of decision-making, and until and unless that is done we shall continue to be weak, the country will continue to be weak. We must, therefore, find a way out.

There is a great need for rapid development and quick growth in the country, especially today, because over the past five or six years we have grown at a faster rate than we had in the past. The aspirations of a large number of people have been awakened and they are seeing things which are almost accessible, but not quite accessible; and unless we are able to make them accessible we are going to have tremendous problems. So, the rate of growth must be accelerated; the need is urgent and cannot be put off. We cannot do this from up here, it has to be done at the grassroots by the panchayats and this will not happen with lecturing by me here or by discussions that may take place at Yojana Bhavan or Krishi Bhavan.

Over the years since Independence, we have created a middle class of almost ten crores of people. Similarly, in the past five years, we have raised ten crore people above the poverty line. This is no small achievement. Today, we have reversed the trends in poverty. At Independence, two-thirds of us were below the poverty line, today almost two-thirds of us are above the poverty line, but still that leaves a lot of people below the poverty line. A few may have joined the richer classes but the majority is still poor who need to be raised up. In spite of two-thirds of the people above the poverty line, there are still millions below the poverty line. So, the challenge is still before us. The expectations, the aspirations are rising very fast and we have really to accelerate our growth rate, co-ordinate all our forces for this growth as best as we can. And this was one reason why we revise the 20-Point Programme. You will have noticed that we have included the revitalising of the panchayats, the co-operatives and the local bodies in the 20-Point Programme. We have also included the administration in general in the 20-Point Programme as we felt that the biggest anti-poverty programme that we could undertake was to revitalise and get a more responsive administration without which no anti-poverty programme can function well. We would like to have your full participation in this.

The Panchayats cover approximately 99 per cent of the rural population but most development and welfare programmes fall outside their purview. What we need first is democratically elected Panchayats. A year ago, I wrote to all our Chief Ministers asking them to hold elections in every State that had not had these elections. Some have taken action and there have been elections but, unfortunately, most of them have still not taken action and we are still waiting for these elections. I hope that they will not delay these elections any further. There is nothing to be afraid of. Some of our Chief Ministers are afraid of holding Panchayat elections. They should not be afraid, they should hold elections and let the democratic process take its due course at the grassroots because that is where they will get their strength from. It is where they will get their responses and feedback from, so that they can remain on the right course and steer their States in the right direction. When we do not have proper elections we open a gap between the State Government and the grassroots level in the rural areas. We must close this gap now. We must institutionalise Panchayat elections. We should be able to have a system where elections to Panchayats take place in a routine way like the elections to the Legislature and Parliament. Only then will we be able to get the democratic process down to the villages, where Gandhiji and Panditji envisaged this process would be built up from. And it is only then that our democracy will acquire its full strength. We have to have decentralised development management with certain constraints that I talked about earlier. We have to have a dynamic, elected grassroots local government, not nominated bodies. Lots of good ideas have come. Unfortunately, they flounder without political and administrative backing and individual interface at the local level. Even a responsive administration is with community clusters and not with individuals. Somehow, we have to tackle these institutions. Only an elected body at the grassroots can respond to the individual problems. Only an elected body will have the strength to raise resources, to train manpower at the grassroots level and then we can also help these elected bodies in whatever way we can.

In the Panchayati Raj Legislation there is ample provision for raising of resources. But, as I said earlier, there is no political will to raise these resources. Without this will there cannot be an involvement of the people in the development process. Panchayats prefer to get State assistance. But can a Panchayat be strong if it is held to ransom by State Government funding? Will the Panchayat be able to give an objective argument on any issue if the financial screw can be turned on the Panchayat? Of course, they cannot. The Panchayats must stand on their own feet which requires a lot of political will. If you are to avoid the pulls and pressures from above, you must be strong on your own. That is really the first step in making Panchayati Raj viable. And you must be able to take that first step.

We also need a lot of training. Training is not a bad word, even if one is grown up. Training and learning go on throughout life. And those who cannot learn throughout life are the ones who drop by the wayside. It is only those who learn from experience, learn from the mistakes of others, learn from the work of others who are able to progress and go ahead. We must have a proper training system in the Panchayats as well for building up local talent, building up local individuals, training them up to be able to cope with the problems that they face in their areas. There is no shame in going back to classes, going back to schools. In the beginning of September, we started a training programme for Central Ministers and other Ministers who went and attended the programme and it was a tremendous success. The Ministers enjoyed it and thought it was beneficial. The others who participated in it also found it very beneficial. This is not just something that you learn but you also give something to others who are involved in the programme. I hope you will take this seriously and bridge the gap that exists at the lower levels, the grassroots level, between the Panchayat and the people. Much greater self-regulation, will be required.

I have just come back from Bengal. They have got Panchayats functioning in almost every village and, on paper perhaps, it is even a model system, but when you go to the villages and talk to the people there, the picture you get is totally different. When I went to the *Adivasi* houses, when I went to the *Harijan* houses, and I asked what had the Panchayat done, the reply was "nothing". Not one person, not one village, could tell me of one piece of work that any Panchayat had done. I drove for over five hundred kilometres, I stopped at numerous villages, I talked to hundreds of people, individually, but not one could say anything. Many complained to me, especially the old women, old men, that the Panchayat had taken their land away or the Panchayat had done something else. Then I asked them for more details because, I said, if, I have to take some action or I have to do something, then you must tell me more. I have toured many States, right from the southern tip to the north, to the east and the west. I found that in this model

Panchayati Raj System, the old people, the frail people, were afraid to talk to me. They said, "No, we cannot tell you because we have to live here. We will come and tell you in Delhi if you like. We can tell some other person quietly but here everybody knows that I am talking, so I will not say anything. "This is not the type of Panchayati Raj I am envisaging. Because, Panchayati Raj could only be good for development if it is able to reach out to the weaker sections, the *Adivasis*, the *Harijans*, the backwards, the depressed, the suppressed; it is only when they feel that the Panchayat is working for them then development will take place. It is not an election which is to be fought with musclemen and a stick. It is an election which will have to be fought very democratically. A lot of thinking should go into it to see that, there is proper representation of those sections which find it hard to get representation in that area because of their weakness or their numbers being small. You have to think about this also. The Panchayati Raj System must be development-oriented, and to achieve all this we really have to look again at the Panchayati Raj System as it exists today and see what are the lacunae and why these weaknesses exist. Perhaps in the discussions later today, we may come out with some positive suggestions which could strengthen the system that exists or change the system if we think a change is required.

We have to start monitoring various projects in different ways. The 20-Point Programme reaches out to the weaker sections and because it reaches to the weakest, because it is really at the grassroots level, we had a lot of problems in its implementation, in verification of complaints and in just seeing that the benefits go where they should. We have started very vigorous monitoring with IRDP. We have independent monitoring of States by voluntary agencies. These agencies are not under the control of any Government or Ministries and we are getting quite a detailed feedback from them. This is only the first stage of a new experiment. We will be developing the process as we go along and I am sure that within a year we will have a very solid monitoring system which does not rely on just Government feedback, but goes to the political representatives, goes to voluntary agencies and gives us information which is traditionally not available to us. We will also see how to extend this sort of monitoring to other areas which we feel are critical. If we take up everything then the process will get diluted again, therefore, we want to take a few areas and concentrate on them.

During my tours of the rural areas, I found a lot of problems because the concept of a programme as it is developed in a sector does not match with the specific problems in that area. From the Centre it is, of course, a generalised programme to cover vast areas, and it cannot be tailored here to match the specific problems of a particular village or a region or zone. This is the sort of task that the Panchayat must take over. Perhaps, we can have a little more flexibility in what we think so that you can use that flexibility to tailor the programmes for the immediate needs of the villages that come under it, perhaps even differently for different areas under one panchayat.

We have to see that the BDO and the VLW work together and in concert with elected representatives of the Panchayat and not as totally independent, authoritarian entities.

Once again, it is only with the people's participation and involvement that we will be able to build the Panchayati Raj System and that we will be able to complete our development programmes the way we would like to do. We must, during your deliberations here, ensure that Panchayati Raj is given its due place and an appropriate operational role. We must also ensure that the powers for development are decentralised, they are made more democratic and the management of our development programmes is such that there is involvement right down to the grassroots level.

Lastly, I congratulate you on your seminar, and give you my good wishes for your Thirteenth National Conference. We look forward to good results, not just lots of words but results when you get back in the rural areas. We will be looking out for those results.

3

Responsive and Representative Administration: Panchayati Raj

Responsive Administration

I would first like to apologise for changing the schedule and starting this exercise a little earlier than anticipated. Something came up in Delhi and it was necessary to reschedule things a little bit, but looking at the flexibility and the dynamism with which our administrators always manage to get things done at the last minute, I thank you for accommodating this.

I have two abiding memories from Bhopal, where we had the first conference of District Magistrates. The first is the impressive dedication to duty of all the Collectors and DMs, exemplified by absence of small and petty complaints about personal problems or individual grievances. To a person, the concentration was on the problems that they faced as administrators, the problems in their official capacity. That is tremendously heartening to see. It shows a tremendous pride in the duties and work that had been entrusted to them and a conscientiousness about discharging those duties.

The second and, perhaps, even stronger impression was of the faith and the belief of the DMs in our democratic institutions and the involvement of the democratic institutions in the development process. This is quite in contrast to the attitudes of administrators 30 years ago, 25 years ago, certainly before Independence, when administrators looked at democratic institutions as meddling in the affairs of development without really knowing about it. The task of development, in their view, was a preserve of the administrator and democratic institutions only interfered in the speed and the value of development that took place. Quite in contrast to that, I found that in our younger generation of administrators there is a totally new perspective of seeing a valid role for the democratic system and, in fact, interacting strongly with it to get the best, the most rapid and, perhaps, the most wholesome development. I found that DMs now readily acknowledge and, perhaps, even enthusiastically seek the harnessing of the people's co-operation in their work. It is only with this co-operation that we can have economic development with social progress, which is really the essence of our development work.

Because of these two characteristics, I am confident that there can be a totally responsive administration.

These workshops are also a demonstration of our Government's commitment to the serious consideration and resolution of the real problems that you face, not personal problems—which we do want to look at, which we are looking at and for which we already have mechanisms to try to solve—but problems that you face in your official capacity, in a sense, your official problems. These seminars are, in a way, demonstrative of our resolve to try to get to the root of these problems and to solve them.

In many ways, our present system is not the most dynamic when it comes to looking at solving problems. We pick the brightest brains in the nation, we train them for a year, perhaps two years, and then we sort of throw them into the wide ocean and for the next 30 or 35 years, we leave them to sink or swim on their own. We don't give you an adequate indication of the direction in which to swim. Every now and then, we have a sort of *ad hoc* evaluation of whether you are swimming well enough, fast enough, or whether you are swimming in the right direction. If we find that you are not, then we clobber you on the head. And of course, clobbering doesn't help you swim any better or faster. It only helps you sink. Now we would like to change that. We would like to improve your swimming, give you direction and, perhaps, increase your speed. That is really what these seminars are about.

The system is also not satisfactory because it demonstrates a lack of care and concern on the part of the Government of your problems in your official capacity, your needs as administrators. Perhaps these seminars will help overcome this attitude of the Government towards itself.

At all levels and in each hierarchy, including the political, our system induces a certain complacency, perhaps even a certain smugness, an intellectual languor and perhaps even a misplaced arrogance. When you are a DM or an Under Secretary, I am sure there is a feeling that as soon as you get to one rank above you, you can solve all the problems. The Under Secretary feels that when he becomes a Deputy Secretary, he can really get to grips with the problem and there will be a solution. The Deputy Secretary feels that when he becomes a Joint Secretary, he can overcome all the problems and the Joint Secretary when he becomes a Secretary. A Secretary feels that perhaps all the problems lie at the political level and if he gets into politics he can, of course, solve everything. Then, when we get to the political level, we think, "My God! What a mess there is at the bottom!"

So, somehow this chain has to be broken. This can only happen if we interact adequately with each other and try to overcome the problems as seen from every level. This has not been happening in the past. This is one of the things we would like to try to do.

Most of all, the present system divorces administrators, perhaps even the political authorities, from not only other administrators but from larger concerns and goals, from our goals as a nation. Our goals go back to our heritage. They are not just something that we define today. Our goals must be defined keeping in mind our heritage, our culture and our traditions. Our goals cannot be mere economic or statistical goals. Goals cannot be 'X' amount of cases under IRDP or under some other scheme, and when you produce it we think that the goal is reached. We must define our goals much better, define them politically and define them administratively. We also have to look at the place that we want for India in the world, in the larger context of humanity. And all that must be reflected in your day-to-day goals, goals which may be very mundane in a way but are part of the greater goal. Unless you see it as part of the greater goal, that drive, that commitment, is not going to be there.

We must look at our system. We are developing too quickly into a very materialistic system of evaluation. Everything seems to be influenced by a very materialistic goal. Can you achieve this? If you don't achieve this, you are going to be penalised in some way, mostly in a material way; you will get a bad posting in today's terms, you will lose emoluments in some way, you will get a bad CR and it will then reflect throughout your career. So, in a sense, you are working from a sense of fear that something will be done to you if you do not perform to a particular level.

I think this is all wrong. You cannot get people to work with adequate drive just by inducing fear or threat as a method of motivation. It must be a commitment to a goal which drives you on. Yes, there can be a negative aspect also to something happening if you do not perform, but if that is the primary method of making you perform, I don't think we can achieve what we are trying to achieve. We must switch from this to a positive commitment. There is enough commitment. I see it at every level, but most of all at the lower levels, where the younger generations are tremendously committed. But, as a government, we do not treat that commitment as a drive. What we try and do is to threaten you thus pushing everything into distortions. Either you go running, looking for patronage—which is, perhaps, the worst thing that can happen to an administration, or other distortions come in. These can only be removed if we change our attitudes, our attitudes from the top down to the administration, but also your own attitudes at your own levels. This, we feel, can only happen with adequate interaction, so that everybody knows what it is all about.

This is where such seminars really do come into their own. We would like to change the system that we have had in the past but change it not by a directive from the top with a limited perspective which then gets us into, perhaps, even worse problems than the present system but to try and get the system itself activated, to get you, at the lower levels, and the administrators at the higher levels to think about these things and let the system itself evolve the answers to problems. We will throw the problems at you. You will throw even more problems at yourselves because you know much more about the problems that you are facing. Then, perhaps, the system itself can evolve the answers and evolve a new system which can cope with changing situations.

The world is changing much too fast for us to have a moribund system which is non-flexible, which cannot evolve and develop with changes in our society, in our country, as they come about in the world. And that is why we *would* like to get back to you, to involve you, first, with each other, so that you learn that there are similar problems in other parts of the country, perhaps even in other parts of your own State. You don't have adequate interaction today even to give the feeling to the administration that it belongs to a nation. We would like to ask you about your problems so that we can know about them.

We would like to listen to what you have to say. And we would like to share our perceptions with your perceptions. We feel that in this way we can have a truly responsive and finely-tuned administration, an administration which responds to changing circumstances, and administrators who are responsible and involved in problems, and whose perspective is neither narrow nor parochial, but national and, perhaps, even international, because in today's shrinking world we cannot isolate anything. Everything is related to what is happening right across the globe. Even your, perhaps very mundane development programmes can be affected by something that happens on the other side of the globe. So this development must be seen in the total perspective.

A responsive administration is tested most at the point of interface between the administration and the people. Therefore, it is essential to hone the cutting edge of the administration. We have always felt that you, at the district level, are the cutting edge of the administration, but it was made very clear to me at Bhopal, and again at Gorakhpur, that at your level, you feel the cutting edge is very much lower, that there are many problems that you face at the cutting edge, which is the BDOs, the *thanedars*, the *patwaris* and the hundreds of others that we have created at that level. The point has been very well taken. But then, we would like to divide the cutting edge into two cutting edges, perhaps like the modern blades, and have them both working together at the district level. Once we get down to the district level, we must have the second edge right there cutting even closer to the surface. So, we really have to look at both the edges. We will look at the district edge, and we will help you look at the lower cutting edge to see that both are honed in the right manner.

You are already chosen few of the nation. You are already trained to a very high degree. You are chosen from the most intelligent groups in the country. It is very easy, perhaps, for us to get down to you and ask you to do certain things, to get a response from you, to get you to interact. But perhaps, it is not so easy to go down to the next cutting edge, where we ask you to go down to the *patwari* and the *thanedar* and ask you to start polishing that edge. We must be able to do both. They must get training at the grassroots level and ensure involvement of the people at the grassroots level. Now, when I am talking of grassroots level, I am talking not of grassroots from our point of view, but the grassroots from your point of view, which is really the village level itself. So we have to work out systems. You must tell us how to work out these systems. Much of it, perhaps, you can do yourselves, by interacting and by giving an input at your level which can change these things. We will help you wherever we can and whenever we can.

One other point that came up at Bhopal was that development is being hampered by the dependency syndrome of the people. The people in general today are just waiting for Government to do something, even waiting for Government to do the simplest things which they can do themselves, which the community itself can do. The system has become so top-heavy and top-oriented that at every level they look to the level above for a solution. Now, we must push this down, not just in the administration but also sometimes out of the administration to the community. It is only then that you will get the involvement of the local community, that you will get the local community to look for self-help and that is what will really help you to get things done at the lower level. How do we enthuse the local community? How do we involve the local community? This is the sort of question that you will, of course, ask yourselves.

You must have already been given the points and the papers that came up from Bhopal and you have probably gone through them. I had asked for them to be sent to you, perhaps a week or 10 days before you came here. I hope you got them in time. (If you did, you must be really fortunate because whenever we try to get such things done for our Parliamentary Committees and other meetings, we are not very successful.) So, I hope that you were much more successful and lucky than we are.

However, I would not like you to be bound by what happened in the earlier groups in Bhopal. That is something for you to go on to develop further and to, perhaps, concretize at this session. But you must also, go beyond. There must be other things left out at Bhopal which you feel are important. Those must come in. If, after the three or four days that you are here, you cannot develop them too much, leave them in a half-developed form. The next group will develop them further, put in their own inputs. This is a sort of continuing exercise in additional inputs while developing on what has been done earlier, by way of an open exercise.

You must not let anybody tie you down in these discussions. You must not feel that there are any hierarchies when you are talking. Everybody must be exactly the same around the table. Even if I am sitting with you, we must talk as one to each other and not up and down. It is only then that there will be proper interaction and proper ideas coming out which can be concretized. It will require a lot of listening by a lot of people. I hope everybody is ready to do that. We are looking forward to this interaction and to the sharing of your experiences. Since Mussoorie, you have probably not had the opportunity to learn from the experiences of others in any systematic manner, especially when it comes from people working in other States and, perhaps, in completely different circumstances. This Workshop provides you with such an opportunity, an opportunity for across-fertilisation of ideas and experiences and personalities. I am sure many suggestions will emerge; which will include those of uniform acceptability and those which are specific to a particular application, in either geographic or economic and social terms or, perhaps, relating to some other limited sphere. But all suggestions will, after vetting and processing, be taken to the implementation stage, I am confident that they will add tangibly to a more responsible administration.

But there is a danger against which we must guard. It is that we must not get bogged down in a pre-occupation with the details of the experiences of the problems you have had. You must view them from a more distant perspective, in a macro picture and then relate your solutions to that, not just solutions to very, very micro problems. Distance yourself a little bit when you look at problems to try and get macro solutions, macro at the district level, not looking from the Delhi point of view. You must not forget to relate those problems to the larger goals of the nation. Administrators are sometimes so involved with what they are doing that they don't make the connection with the larger issues. To them I would like to give E.M. Forster's injunction: "Only connect! Those who don't connect remain cogs in the wheel and those who do connect make up the wheel itself and move forward."

Our larger goals are democracy, secularism, socialism and peaceful co-existence—between communities within the nation and the world community as a whole—and non-alignment. The greater goal must be India's contribution to the development of humanity, to world civilisation. India has always stood apart in contributing to this, and we cannot be falling behind now. That must link to your day-to-day work. You cannot separate the two. Your goal must always be a much higher goal and then, within that goal, you must strive for the limited task that you have been given towards achieving that greater goal. On your success or failure in the task assigned to you will depend upon our success or failure in the greater goal for the nation. You must view your work in this perspective. Let us consider each of these in turn and I will relate them to your work.

First, *democracy*. In 40 years of Independence, we have had eight general elections and scores of assembly elections. We have conclusively established that democracy is the only viable system for India and that our unity is based on diversity because it is that that gives us our democratic strength. However, our institutions of democracy are stronger at the higher levels. At the lower levels, much still needs to be done. There they are too weak. The will of the people is more manifest in Parliament than it is in the Gram Sabhas and the Zila Parishads, not because there is any inherent weakness but because, at the grassroots level, elections have not been regular or consistent. We have acquiesced in long and frequent spells of non-representative local government. We want you to further develop and flesh but the connections between representative local government and responsive administration. These were sketched out by many at Bhopal. You must consider the ticklish issue of the relationship between the political authority at the lower levels and the district administration.

There is another aspect of Indian democracy. Given our scale of economic and social disparities, we must thwart any oppressive tyranny of the elected majority over the poorer and the weaker sections or linguistic and religious minorities. They need special safeguards against social prejudice, against economic discrimination, especially when social prejudice or religious prejudice and economic discrimination is masqueraded as the people's will. We have safeguards in the Constitution. We have safeguards in our legislation. But such safeguards are not adequate. They have to be transformed into social attitudes, into changed social attitudes. A lot needs to be done here. The administration needs to do a lot, but even more than that the political structure at the lowest level needs to do a lot more. And, perhaps, interaction between the political system and the administration at the lower levels is what can achieve progress in this area. We might say that the function of the legislatures is making democracy real, and the function of the administration, especially at the lowest level, must be to make it more meaningful.

Second, *secularism*. The meaning of secularism is becoming increasingly complex, and more so because of the processes of our economic development. The change, the mobility that this is bringing about, is engendering group rivalries. The processes of social change are causing uprooting of communities, the disruption of the set system, perhaps even an alienation of certain groups. In other words, progress poses its own challenges to the mind and to the spirit, to morale and perhaps most, to morality. Some respond to material progress by becoming cross materialists. Some others respond more dangerously. They give simple answers to very complex problems, simple answers to be found through fanaticism, fundamentalism, or communalism. What is needed is the golden mean between the pursuit of national progress and continuity through traditional values, the golden mean of Truth and Non-violence, tolerance and compassion, of one humanity and one family of nations. We must look for that. This must be the greater goal that we are striving for. This is what Gandhiji's message was really all about. This must be India's message to the world today. Economic development is essential if India is to compete and be strong enough. But if we develop only economically we will be no different from the others who are today in a materialist race, forgetting the deeper human values, causing tremendous stress and strain within their own societies. India has always striven for much higher ideals and goals, and India must do that today. We have to go back to the basic thinking and the basic concepts and postulates and then build, derive our own parables for today.

The economic goals and objectives must be matched with similar goals and objectives for humanity as a whole, for the world as a whole, so that life becomes more fulfilling and not just materially better but less fulfilling because that is the road that we are on today. We are bargaining fulfilment, which is there amongst the poor people in our villages today, for development. In fact, fulfilment is there amongst the poorest and is missing from those who have seen economic development. You go to a very poor family. They are happy with nothing. You go to a middle-class family. They are unhappy with much more. Now, is that the right exchange that we want? We want to give them much more but we should not make them unhappy with that. So we need a lot of thinking on how we are going to match these. It is easier to match them when the rate of economic development is slow. The faster our rate of economic development, the more the challenges, the bigger the challenges. The challenge is more for you because you are the ones who are dealing with this at the grassroots level. This is how I would like you to try and look at the tasks that you have to do.

So, for a truly responsive administration, secularism is both a question of law and order and the response to the communal menace. You should display the ability to persuade people to abandon their base attitudes and look at things in a much broader, bigger perspective, to build on well-tried principles of good fellowship, to see ourselves as a family. There are differences in a family, there are differences in points of view within a family but they argue it out, they find ways of working to resolving these issues. They don't at least one hopes they don't go to violent means of resolution. But this is what we tend to do in our family as a Nation. This tendency is there not just because different communities are there, because different languages are there. These differences are perhaps accentuated because we are trying to get various communities together. Just think about it. I want to throw the ideas at you without developing them. No other nation in the world is striving to bring communities together. They are all homogeneous in themselves. It is only India that is heterogeneous and is trying to bring communities together in a democratic manner. It is an example to the whole world, to the world community, to live together, in a more democratic manner and in a system based on values. How do we translate this first into our own system? How do we develop that system so that we can present it to the world as a viable system? The cutting edge again is you. How we can do it, and how well we do it is really in your hands. In brief, a responsive administration is an administration which creates and sustains an ethos of *sarva dharma sambhava*.

Third, *socialism*. Socialism has been cited in our Constitution. It is not a foreign ideology to India. It is not based on the perceptions and experiences of others. Our socialism is derived from our own heritage, developed to meet our needs, and based on the values that have been espoused in our freedom struggle. Sometimes there are attempts to distort our view of socialism by imported ideologies and imported sorts of socialism. They will not work in India. The Indian people are much too independent for that. Indian civilisation is much too deeply ingrained in our society for it to be changed by imported thought in this manner. It has never happened in our history. Yes, a lot of thought has come in. It has been taken into our system, synthesised into our system. It has been absorbed into our system. But it has never been forced into our system. And, whenever there have been attempts to force imported ideology into our system they have been rejected. Our society, our civilisation, has rejected them. That will happen even now. So we must take whatever is the best in the world and absorb it, synthesise it into our own system. That is what our socialism is all about.

Our socialism is based on the ethical perception that all humanity is a single family—*Vasudhaiva Kutumbakam*—one big family without any walls, narrow walls or barriers separating it, where the stronger members have an obligation to the weaker members. This is, totally the converse of many other societies, where the basic postulate is that the stronger must crush the weaker and the weaker must fight back. Ours is the reverse. And that is what has given us our strength for 5,000 years. We seek to ensure that the needs of all are met, that equality of opportunity is available, that special facilities are there for socially or otherwise disadvantaged sections. These ethical perceptions provided the basis for Gandhiji's concepts and his ideology of the freedom struggle. But those principles were not limited to the freedom struggle. They were aimed well beyond political independence. They were aimed at the social and economic emancipation of our country, at the world community. Panditji, on his part, effected the important synthesis between Marxian scientific socialism and India's reality. Therefore, there exists an authentic Indian Socialist response to the particular problems of Indian poverty and Indian development. In our view, socialism places the individual at the core of the development process. It cannot mean just better statistics. It must mean a better life for the human being.

It must mean a better human being. As we define development, it is not just a matter of economic growth or statistics. Yes, we will chase you about the numbers; we will ask for completing various programmes. But you must remember that, in the completion of the programmes, it is the human being who is at the root of the matter. You must not get so carried away by our asking you to deliver numbers that you give us distorted numbers. By "distortion", I do not mean that you are trying to cheat us or that you are fudging the numbers. By "distortion", I mean completing the task in a manner that is not meaningful to the human being there. The tasks must be completed, the statistics must be completed in a manner that is meaningful to the human being whose life you are there to improve. This is the root of our socialism.

It is in this perspective that we are giving the foremost priority to the removal of poverty through the intervention of the State, through programmes of poverty amelioration and poverty eradication. Hence, the tremendous importance given to the 20-Point Programme, and the other anti-poverty programmes, that are being delivered by you directly at the doorsteps of the poorest people. You administer the IRDP and the rural employment programmes. We would like to hear from you how we can make these programmes more meaningful—meaningful for the people whose lives they are to affect, whose lives they are to change, not just meaningful in terms of presentation to the Planning Commission and the Central Government as statistics, very dry, cut-and-dried statistics. We would like to hear from you about how to change the statistics that we are asking for, that we are measuring, so that these programmes are made meaningful, so that they give you more fulfilment in your job of meeting those statistics. Talking to many at the last Conference at Bhopal, and then again talking to the DMs in UP, I got the impression that when we put pressure on you to implement a particular programme, the IRDP for example, in the rush to complete the statistics, the depth in which you go into each case is sometimes not good enough. And they have been honest enough to say that when we really put the pressure on you saying by such and such date we must have "X" amount done or such and such percentage done, then you are under pressure to complete the task and not to complete that task well. Now, how do we change this? We would not like to remove the pressure from you, let me not say that we would not like to keep the pressure on you to complete it, but we would like you to add something more meaningful to the completion of that task. Is it not easy to marry the two? But, perhaps, inputs from your level will help us to do that.

Another very important area that has been worrying me very much is district planning. I am sure it worries you too as it has been flagged at the last two meetings. Now that we are going into the Eighth Plan, I think this is the time that we must think about it. How do we devolve planning down to the district level? We cannot devolve planning down to the district level, if adequate infrastructure, trained infrastructure, is not available at district level to give a good input to the plan. At the same time, there must be a balance between the district's perceptions and the State's perceptions. I would even say that, perhaps sometimes the State's perceptions are not as important as geographic or socio-economic problems of an area, perceptions which could even cross State boundaries. For example, coastal areas have very similar problems. You cannot divide them by State boundaries. Bundelkhand in UP and MP have absolutely the same problem. You cannot say it is different here and different there. So, these sorts of ideas must also come in. The greater national perspective must be there. But unless we are able to evolve the planning from the district level together with implementation of the planning process down to the district level, we are going to have in the Eighth Plan the same problems that we have had in the Seventh Plan. We make tremendous decisions in the Plan, then hope it trickles down. But as the commitments to particular goals are less at every level the whole thing gets so diffused, that the Planning Commission is talking about one thing, the State Government is talking about something else, the politicians are talking about something else again, the district administration wants to do something else. And, in the end, nothing really effective is done; everything gets spread so thinly that nothing really fructifies and we don't get the fruits of our expenditure for much too long. The only way to break through all this is to, first, involve everyone down to the lowest level, in the planning process and then see that responsibility for the implementation of that is handed back to that level. I have said, perhaps, beyond what would be required, but I really want you to think of this and give us positive inputs, so that we can try and put some of that thinking into the Eighth Plan. I don't now how much we can do, how much NDC would want to do or how much we would like to do in the Eighth Plan. Perhaps, we will have to push some ideas on the Ninth Plan. So do it in a graded way, really want some inputs on this from you.

We have a lot of anti-poverty programmes but perhaps, from my point of view, the biggest and most important anti-poverty programme is our Education Programme because without that, there can be on getting rid of poverty. If the poor remain uneducated, if the coming generations of the poor remain uneducated or poorly educated, they are handicapped from the word 'go'. That is why we have put so much emphasis on education. We are just getting the first statistics of the type of enrolment that is taking place in the sarvodaya schools. It is very interesting. There was a tremendous fear, an elitist fear that these schools are elitist and they will be taken over by the elite. I have forgotten the exact numbers but if I remember correctly 60 per cent of the students come from the poorest category. So, you can imagine what was happening before we introduced these schools. This vast section of highly intelligent children was being lost to the nation, because they just did not have the strength to get educated. Unless we are able to reach down to get the best we cannot get the maximum speed of development in the nation.

Education has to be the core, but education must be targeted towards our economic development. The type of education that we are having is white-collar oriented. It is really tailored to produce unemployment. The whole system is disoriented. These are the things that we must address ourselves to.

Our next biggest anti-poverty programme is agriculture. It has to be agriculture, no matter how much we spend on things like IRDP, NREP, RLEGP and all these other programmes. Agriculture is the programme that really cuts at poverty. Education must be related to that. If the largest number of people are involved in agriculture then education must be related to agriculture. Now, 'related to agriculture' does not necessarily mean related to just sowing seeds and harvesting. There are many areas of agriculture, not just again covering what our agricultural universities are covering, but down streams, from food-processing to marketing of agricultural produce. Unless we go into these areas now, our farmer will not be able to sell his produce at remunerative rates. That means the whole thrust of the Green Revolution will be lost. We must spread out into other areas. The farmer must be made more flexible. Now, all this will only happen with correct education at that level. So, this is another area that we must look at, and again where we are looking to you for a feedback.

Then, education must also give an incentive. I said earlier that one of the problems is that the people are always looking to you and looking to us for everything, even the tiniest thing. Again, education is responsible for this. We must educate people to have much more initiative. We must educate the community, our society, to start looking after itself also. Yes, our society is very poor. But, if we go back, our society was much poorer four generations ago. Yet, four generations ago there was the community spirit. People did work for the community. They thought of what they could do for the community. Today, that is gone. We cannot really develop adequately without that spirit. Education must be one of the key factors in bringing it back. Again, with incentive must come diversification of the economy, diversification of what our people do in industry. Increasingly, industry is becoming State-controlled which is good in certain areas, is equally bad in other areas. Again, we must establish the proper balance.

Expanding the public sector is crucially important to maintaining India's Independence. Without the strategic needs supplied by the public sector, a country in the stage of development that India is today cannot be stable and strong. So that is a need and it must be done and we will do it. But equally important is efficiency in the system. If the system is not efficient, it cannot give you the strength that is required. It cannot be the backbone that is required to strengthen the nation and to sustain the nation through a difficult period, and these are again areas that you must think about—public sector efficiency. When I talk of the public sector, I am really talking of all public activity including what you deliver, which, in a range, is strictly outside the PSUs but is still public work done by the Government. Efficiency is most important. Innovativeness, dynamism must be brought in. We are already getting to a stage where the cost of delivery is becoming so high that soon, we will not be able to deliver the programmes at all. We are spending certainly two-thirds of the cost of a programme on the delivery mechanism rather than on the programme itself. Surely, the people will not support this for too long. They will put up with it for perhaps a decade, perhaps two decades more. But if this cost is going to increase to 80-90 per cent of the programme, then surely, people are not going to put up with it. Something will have to be done about it. Now, again, this is an area that you must look at. You must see how we can cut through this red tape, these cobwebs, to make the system much more efficient.

As growth and development proceed, as our society changes, as our economy becomes stronger, our socialism must adapt to that. We must go back to the basic postulates and re-apply them to the changed situation. A responsive administration recognises these evolving changes and evolves appropriate answers.

Fourth is the question of Non-alignment. The tendency amongst our district officers, indeed, of the civil service and our population as a whole is to regard our foreign policy as far removed from our daily problems. Why, it is asked, spend so much time and energy; on fighting for Disarmament, on arguing about Non-alignment in particular. What may look like very technical arguments of the Foreign Office on particular issues which are really, in the micro view, are relevant to tube-wells for drinking water, for agriculture, or your daily problems. The fact is that in the world in which we are living today, communication and interaction between nations is such that everything relates to everything else. I am not thinking or suggesting for a moment that you spend 80 per cent of your time on foreign policy, but you must be aware of the meaning of that in your daily work and how it affects your work. Most of all, peaceful co-existence in the world is essential for any development work to take place. If there is no peace, if there are tensions, resources are diverted—not just financial resources but also human resources. For example, if there was less tension in our area, in our region, we would not have to spend such vast amounts on defence. We would not have to divert so much effort and energy to our security. All that could be deployed into economic development, social development, but we can't do so because there are tensions. So, foreign policy is directly relevant to what is available to you in terms of human resources and material resources.

In a similar way, basically like I said earlier, we cannot divorce the greater goals of the nation from the immediate targets of economic development. Both must go together. First the betterment of the human being, of the human race. Together with that, development: economic and other development. Disarmament relates directly to resource availability. Today, over a trillion dollars a year are being spent on military purposes in the world. If my calculation is correct, that translates to something like two-and-a-half crores a minute in the world. Now imagine what that can mean to economic development. But, of course, all of it is not going to be available to you. Much of it is in the developed countries, in the industrialised countries. But what it will do is it will stabilise their economies. Today the world's economies are in a mess. Ours is going through a very difficult period. Why? Because the developed countries' economies are in a mess. They are overspending on defence. The US economy is not stabilising. If that does not stabilise, economies of all other countries are going to be unstable.

So, all these things relate directly to you. We cannot divorce them from direct economic development work at the grassroots level even if we look at it in the most materialistic and mundane manner. Most of all, on our foreign policy depends our independence, our security, our sovereignty and, equally, *our* self-respect in the world. Now, all that is as much part of building a nation as your work in a village in the remotest corner of the country, is part of building the nation. Unless all of it happens together we will not have a nation at the end of our work. So, we must see the picture as a whole.

This series of Workshops of District Magistrates, Deputy, Commissioners and Collectors is proving in one way much more productive than we had initially envisaged. A lot of new ideas are coming up, a lot of, interesting perceptions and a sense that the problems and the prospects for overcoming those problems are much clearer at the district level than we sometimes find at the State headquarters or in Delhi.

On the other hand, there are definitely some problems too, that have come up by our holding these Workshops. You must yourself have felt that there is a sort of resistance building up as to why we are talking to DMs; people are asking why should this be done?

There is a resistance to all new approaches. We have to face this resistance. I am very clear that the positive aspects of what we are getting from these Workshops are very much greater than any negatives that may come. What is also interesting is the quarters from which the resistance comes. There is, of course the political angle which people are trying to throw into it. But because we had perceived that there might be such a political reaction, we have tried to be very, very 'proper' about these Workshops and kept politics, or Centre State relations for that matter, absolutely out of any discussions that take place in these Workshops.

Interestingly, there is also resistance from other echelons in the bureaucracy. I don't know what they think that we will do or you will do together. But I am very clear that if we, at the decision-making level, are to get the right inputs then we should try and get them as unfiltered as possible. From our point of view, that really means at the DM or district level. We still think that the district leve1 is the cutting edge, although I know that at the district level you feel that the cutting edge is much below. But, from our point of view, this is one of the most important levels, and we really want, a lot of interaction and input from you. The objective is to build a consensus to solve the problems that we all are facing. It is a slow process. We must persist do this path that we have taken. It is the only way I feel that we will be able to get India out of the sluggishness in its growth. The potential is tremendous but, somehow, we have not been able to channelise and put it all in one direction, without too much pulling in various direction.

If we are to build India into a live and vibrant society, into a system that is alive or active enough to question itself, to reach out in new directions, we need this type of interaction. At the same time, conservatism because it is with the correct mix of both that we will find the right way out of the problems that we are facing.

This Workshop is at the mid-point of this particular exercise. We still have, if I remember rightly, two more Workshops to go. We feel that much of what started off as just a very coarse idea, which had some, we have already started acting, on others, like district the ball rolling. But there is a lot of resistance along the way. We have brought three samples of what the Planning Commission has by way of District Plans. Nobody is really very happy with them. But we though that we would throw at you the best that we could lay our hands on, while reminding you that the best is nowhere near acceptable and a lot more needs to be done if district planning is to be a reality.

Many in the first Workshop, and then many more DMs in the second Workshop, started questioning the functioning of the whole system, the administrative system in the country, not just the IAS but the whole bureaucracy. What is, I think, good and revealing is that the system itself is questioning the methods that have been traditionally followed, the road along which things have turned a bit at a time. Perhaps you could also think about these things. We must also relate the larger national goals I have covered in Bhopal, then again in Hyderabad to the more specific issues of administration. I don't really want to go through the whole thing again, the basic goals of democracy, of secularism, of socialism, of non-alignment. I won't try and go into the details at all but what is important is that at every level of administration there must be an understanding of our basic policies. I have no doubt that there is. But there must also be a basic understanding of why those policies have been evolved and what we are trying to achieve with them. Too often today our goals seem to be limited to economic goals, even the tasks we set for you. What do we ask you to do? We ask you how many wells you have dug; what percentage of this programme or that programme you have achieved. That is all very well. It is necessary. But, behind that, there must be a basic realisation of the ideology, the philosophy from which it flows.

For example, what is the role that India must play in the international community? Now that is not something which should really be left to the Foreign Office boys as a sort of closed department of the IFS. It cannot be. It is what is in the mind and the heart of the country that is reflected in international policy. If the country does not have the will to follow a particular international policy, then we will not be able to do it, no matter how independent we might want to be. The crux of the issue is independence of action and a better deal to humanity, not just in India but right across the world. And that flows from Gandhiji's basic postulates of Truth, of Non-violence, of no division between caste and community or religion or country or race, for that matter. These are all artificial barriers that we have built. If we are to break these barriers, we need to believe in it ourselves first.

A country like India can only stand as an international power. We don't have any intention of being an international power in the sense of coveting power but certainly in terms of thinking, in terms of ideals, in terms of economic strength. India must be at the forefront. We can only be at the forefront if there is a basic change in world attitudes. If it is divided into blocs, there will always be two blocs. And the more independent thinking countries, the Non-aligned countries, won't get an opportunity then to come up. Their economic development opportunities are blocked. So, in a sense, on the one hand, your work, the roots of the thinking at the district level, at the grassroots level, gives us the strength for independent action in foreign policy by maintaining our independence. On the other hand, only with a much stronger foreign policy and independent action can we make the tools available to you to be more effective at the grassroots level, whether it is by way of economic support or new technologies or new science. Unless there is this flow both ways, we will be left behind. So there can be no separation between foreign policy and domestic policy. It is all part of one package. I would like you to keep this in mind when we talk of national integration, of ending communalism, of fighting fundamentalism. How is it to be fought? Is it to be fought by the police? By guns, perhaps, by new weapons for riot control or whatever? Or is it to be fought in the hearts and minds of men? You have to fight it in both places. You are not in a position where you can suddenly switch over from one to the other. But the real fight is not with guns and *lathis* and shields, the real fight is with ideas. It is with thinking.

That is the way you must be the key movers, not just because you are DMs and have joined the IAS or the State services, but because you are the very limited number of our intelligentsia which is residing in the rural areas. Everybody else who is going to give the leadership in thinking runs away. You must give this leadership also. And you must be provocative in this. It is not just a question of selling an idea. It is a question of developing a philosophy, the roots of which have been laid by Gandhiji, by Panditji, by our founding fathers. We must go to the roots of that but model the interpretation or the use of that to today's conditions—today's conditions in the district, in the country, and internationally. I would like you to really think of yourselves as just much more than somebody posted out to complete the 20-Point Programme or to fill up the various proformas that we keep demanding of you, or any other real routine task. You must be the key or the prime mover in a district for building the nation.

The nation was not built the day we signed the Constitution. The Constitution is the basis on which we are building it, and you are there, in the districts building brick by brick. Unless you build strongly and lay the really solid foundations that are required, we cannot fulfil the Constitution. So, I would just like to repeat that you must think of your role as much greater than just the mere roles of administering a district. It is only when you have that feeling in you that you will really be able to work the way that I certainly would like you to work. I hope that these Workshops will give a new thrust in this area.

Back to the more mundane. In the earlier Workshops, one of the important things that have come up is the relationship between a more responsive administration, which is what the Workshops are for, and a good democratic local government. I think the emphasis there must be on "democratic" because many local governments today are not really democratic. There is, of course, the blatantly undemocratic nominated Zila Parishads, with a nominated chairman. There is also the much more subtle method, where you have an elected man but the powers have been taken away and given to some nominated or appointed person. So, while the one may look better on paper and the other may not look so good, the fact is that neither is really good. We must build a very good responsive system which you can relate to. Unless the administrator in the district has a good political body to react with or interact with, it is very difficult for him to be really effective. Also, if you are to be effective in other areas beyond just administration, in the really deeper areas of nation-building, of ending communalism, fundamentalism, of breaking the barriers, whatever barriers there may be, of caste, or religion or region or language or whatever—then it is all the more important that there be a good political body for you to interact with. That can only come about by having proper elections to local bodies.

We have been trying to push for this. I must admit that we have had very limited success when it comes to really measuring the quantity of democracy which has really been devolved. But I think the direction has been set. In the coming one-and-a-half years, we should be able to have elections in just about all the regions in the country. And that would help you in your task.

One of the fears that keeps being thrown up when we talk of elections at the local bodies and zila level is that the stronger groups, whoever they may be in a village or district, tend to take over and the weaker sections are just bullied and forced to do various things. But, after listening to the DMs in the last two sessions and talking with them, I have a feeling that there is a stronger opinion that if you do have regular elections, then elections at the local level really break across these barriers. Barriers which politicians and people at higher levels tend to build really get demolished at the local level. Perhaps this could also be another tool that we could use to break these traditional barriers. Perhaps, "platform" is a better word than barriers because we call them barriers but use them more as platforms. Perhaps this could be another way to break these sectarian or parochial platforms that we build.

One other major thing that comes out of these Workshops is the ability to interact amongst yourselves from which we don't necessarily want to derive anything but we would like you to have an opportunity to interact, to exchange ideas, to throw your problems at each other, perhaps your solutions at each other and see how some problems could be solved, how a solution could, perhaps, have been better if it had been done in another way, compare solutions to the problems that you have faced. Well, from that, automatically, a new ethos will be built. Perhaps four days are not enough for you to get to know each other well enough, to really talk openly when you have been in a system which has been built in very sealed boxes with no interaction, either vertically or horizontally, across State boundaries. It may not be that easy initially. That was one reason why we increased the length of these Workshops so that it would give you a little time to open out to each other. But perhaps we can continue this exercise, not finish with just the five Workshops which will end by May or June this year. We would continue it, and in that continuity we will build enough knowledge about each other to be able to speak much more freely. Information will then really flow, like it should be flowing.

The second major thing that has come out of the Workshops is that local level democracy needs local level or district level planning.

I just mentioned this in passing earlier but here a lot of work has to be done. We have set the ball rolling with the mid-term review of the Seventh Plan, the Action Plan for agriculture. Agriculture, as you are all aware, has not done as well as the rest of the Plan. We have already got detailed district plans for 169 districts in the agricultural sector. Again, it is not as detailed as I would have liked it.

We don't necessarily want the details in Delhi, but the details must be there at district headquarters. You must have the information available to make your decisions. That also is not good enough at the moment. I am not trying to say this as a way of apportioning blame to any individual either at the district level or at the Centre, but of the system as it has developed. We are just not bothered enough about these things. It is time that we started thinking seriously about how our planning should go into the next phase of development.

One obvious direction is district planning. For that we need a lot of inputs, again not in Delhi but at the district level. We need statistical inputs. Even more important than that, we need intellectual inputs. These are just not available in sufficient quantity or quality at the district level. I am not implying that the DMs are not intelligent and can't cope with it, but the capability for planning, the expertise is not here. There are not enough engineers, there are not enough statisticians, there are not enough of anything available. What is there are normal people who have just sort of risen step by step up along the system and are not innovative and don't have a mind flexible enough to think in new concepts.

So, if we are going to have good district planning, we have to see how we can get the people back out of the big towns and the districts. It is no use their coming to the district for two weeks to work on the Plan. It is not going to work that way.

Local people do develop, but they tend to leave the districts and go to the major metros. The system must be such that local people develop in these various fields, to somehow keep them in the districts or perhaps, get people back to the districts from the metros so that we can have this expertise available. When I look at the question of economic development, the major problem that I feel I am facing at the Centre is the rivalry between genuine economic development and populism. How are we going to break that? The easiest thing for us at the Centre is to become populist. For a few years, everything will go very well. Then, somebody will have to answer for it. The only way I feel that we can really break this vicious circle of populism is to start the thinking process in earnest at the district level.

The minute you start thinking in earnest and in seriousness about what development really is, and what will give real benefits, not passing or illusory benefits, but real benefits, I am sure our people are intelligent enough and have the inherent wisdom to take the right decisions. Today that process is not happening in the rural areas, perhaps not even at the district level with the intensity with which we would like to see it happen.

In a sense, I can say that I have a vested interest in seeing this thinking process and the planning process start at the district level because that is where building the real strength of the country will start. We will then get out of this vicious circle of populism. I don't think we can pretend that it will entirely disappear. But, at least if the balance is restored and the majority thrust goes into real solid long-term development, then we will be able to face this tidal wave which is hitting us at the moment, and save the country from a vicious circle of populism which can only end in disaster, disaster for any country but certain disaster for a country like India.

I have already given very clear instructions to the Planning Commission, and they have started work on the Eighth Plan. The Eighth Plan will be built from the district level upwards and not from Delhi down to the district level. We have already told them categorically to do so.

Now comes the crunch. When they start asking questions,

not enough people are ready with numbers, with figures, with statistics, with inputs. So, we would like that two years of the Seventh Plan to be used as, perhaps, a test period to see what we can achieve in this direction. I would like the first year of the Eighth Plan to start with good district planning. Certainly, it must not go beyond the second year of the Eighth Plan. And this, of course, will depend entirely on how successful you are at the district level. Once we talk of district planning, we are really relying very much on you to deliver. And not to deliver just numbers. Numbers are very easy to throw up. I will give you an example. We were at a Parliamentary Consultative Committee meeting. One of the MPs said, what is all these statistics that you people talk about? His brother was the DM in one of the districts and the State Government had written to him asking about poultry farms, about how many chickens there were in his district. He ignored the first request. He ignored the second request. He received the third request on the day that this MP was sitting there in his office. He just wrote down a number. He said that there were 2,00,700 chickens in his area, and sent it. This MP was a little taken aback. He asked him what he was doing, and the DM replied, who is going to come and count the chickens in my district?

So, statistics just for the sake of statistics are no good. They must relate to what we want to do. The problem really starts at the Central level because we ask for the wrong things. We always ask for the wrong things. And when we ask for a wrong thing you do the wrong things. You give us the statistics, and they don't really mean anything. Other DMs have told me that they do things to fill the statistics, to get the targets that have been set. But they know themselves that what they are doing is not really as beneficial as perhaps this could be. Yes, because the number has been set and you have been asked to do something, you do, it. It doesn't even necessarily give us the result that we are looking for.

Take family planning, for example. What do we ask for? The number of operations, the number of protected couples. But we seldom seem to ask for the birth rate. Now, what are we really worried about, the number of protected couples or the number of operations? If we ask for the wrong thing, you give us the wrong thing. So, this whole thing has got to be rectified.

It can't be rectified straightaway. It will take a little while to get things back on track again. But it must start at every point and at every level. If we all put our minds to it and stall sorting out these things, automatically things will start working out in a much more positive way.

We have brought here three draft district plans from the Planning Commission which they have felt are amongst the better district plans that they have got. At the same time, the questions that are asked are devastating and show how much is lacking in the district plans that we have brought.

The Planning Commission have made their own comments on these plans. So, we have brought the plans to ask you what you think about them, to get some input from you as to how you feel about them, the questions that you would like to raise. These will all then go in as inputs for building the Eighth Plan.

If we can get it right, right at the beginning, then we won't be floundering around in the first few years trying to sort things out. So, you must be absolutely unabashed and open about what you feel about them, what you feel should be done, and what more can be done. Only, if you are absolutely open, will we get the right input. If you let yourselves be a little hesitant, then we will not get the input that we need, we will get some sort of half-baked thing which you will then have to deal with. So the problem really will be much more severe for you. It is better that you let us have it now, rather than that we let you have it later. This is really a first and very tentative exercise. We will build upon this. We will continue this work. But we do want a very complete input from you.

At the beginning of the Workshops, we found that the DMs were having very serious problems in two different ways with the bureaucracy at the lower levels. Firstly, in the quality of the person and his ability to cope with problems, his training levels, his motivation levels. Secondly, in the hierarchical system. What was once a very well-defined system of who was the boss and how the things would run has now, I think, divided up into some 14 different parallel organisations in some districts, perhaps less in some others. Fourteen seems a very substantial amount to cope with if everybody is pulling in different directions. On these two areas we really need a lot of thinking.

Some DMs have done individual work in trying to increase the motivation and improve the qualification levels of the various groups. Some have been quite successful. Some have not been so successful. But, either way, the exercises have really been isolated in districts. Not only that, they have been limited to the particular DM. One DM comes, he does something, it works. These DMs are there for a very short period. It works for that short period, then the DM is transferred and the whole thing collapses. So some thinking is needed here. I don't think we should in anyway try to have a system which would be uniform but, perhaps, with just more interaction between yourselves, you can start building a system which is related to reality. We do not need a standardised system because these things always will be related very much to the local environment in the district and the individuals who are there. But some sort of continuity can remain even when there are transfers and different postings.

Another very difficult area in motivation is public motivation. Too much of the burden of development is falling on government. It is not that the government wants to shirk that responsibility, but when it rests so much on government the people lose interest in their own development. A certain lethargy comes in. That too must be broken. In the old days, there was a lot of interaction between voluntary organisations, not necessarily of the highly organised type that we have got now-a-days but of local, small ones. Schools used to be run. People used to contribute to make roads, to put *kharanja*. All that is gone now. Now everybody waits for government to even come and sweep outside their doorsteps. Nobody, no country, can develop like this. We cannot build a nation which is built on somebody else doing your work, somebody else taking your responsibility. Yes, government has and must have certain bigger responsibilities. But if you start getting involved in the nitty-gritty then you just will not have time to do the real work that you have got to do. So, we must involve the people in some way.

The second question is that of who is in charge. This is a very difficult and delicate area. I don't want to step out too far on it. I would rather let you do the stepping out, and just give you an opening to start thinking about it. Very clearly there are problems if a district does not have one head of the administration. If there is no one focus in the administration, there are going to be problems. There are problems today. How do we get out of this? Who should be there? How senior should he be? Is this career pattern the best career pattern? Are the districts more important than the secretariat or are the districts less important than the secretariat? Who should be sitting where? And should we have very senior people at the district level? What is the importance of the district? Middle level? Or a more junior level? All these things need thinking and of course, it flows from the question of who is to be in charge here.

I feel that it is necessary that we must have an administration at the district level which focuses at one point. The first question that comes up is who is in charge and who should be the head? What is the relationship of the Head of Administration to the elected local body? What is its relationship to the State Body? Should we envisage a local government as comprising an elected body with an administrative Head, a sort of mini-Chief Secretary?

Certainly, the way the system is drifting today, it cannot cope with the challenges that lie ahead. I think most of us are fairly clear about this.

On the anti-poverty programmes I won't sily much. A lot has already been said. They are our key-thrust areas and of great importance but, at the same time, they are not the only anti-poverty programmes. This must be remembered. Agriculture is perhaps the biggest anti-poverty programme because that is where the whole thing is really being generated.

The other point is that somehow, the anti-poverty programmes have also been divided up into two categories. There is the handout category and there is the build up category. A handout category is very necessary but it is necessary only for that strata which is much too weak to make use of a build up category. Yet we find that this handout category is now stretching across the board. So those who are really in need are not getting it. New thinking is required on this also. Perhaps, again, the key is the questions that we ask and the targets that we set for you. Perhaps more flexibility is needed, more freedom of action, a little elbow-room at district level.

This was pointed out in one of the earlier Workshops. I have already given instructions that in the hundred-per cent-Centre-financed programmes, this freedom will be given to you. We could get into a little bit of problem in the combined Centre-State programmes because there we don't quite know how to deal with this but Delhi and your State capitals will try and sort that out also.

We have set the directions. I am sure that this will help you also. But on all these programmes we need much more involvement from you in updating, fine tuning our programmes. In Delhi everybody pretends that they know everything but the distance is too great. I don't know how this happens as everybody who is now in Delhi was in a district once.

Lastly, I want to go back to what I started, with the national goals. Why are we here? What did we fight to get our Independence for? Was it just for *roti, kapda aur makan,* or is there something more beyond? Are we going to be happy with only *roti, kapda aur makan?*

There is some very basic thinking that we have to do on this. We cannot lose our threads with our civilisation in the run of economic uplift or economic gain. We cannot break with our heritage. We cannot lose our traditions, our culture. That thread must continue. I do not think it would be a good bargain if we can give drinking water, roads, schools and industries and, in exchange, we lose that ethos that has kept India, India; if we lose the spirituality that has made India, India.

There are deeper things that we must protect and preserve as part of our civilisation. In doing this, much of the responsibility must also fall on your shoulders. Gandhiji, Panditji, Indiraji have given us the direction. It is all there. We must interpret it correctly and in keeping with the time. That is the important issue.

Too often we grab a particular interpretation of a philosophy made forty years ago, and we apply it to today and it doesn't work. We have to go back to the basic thinking. Think for yourself and then apply it to today. Then it will work for us. It means much more effort in not just carrying on what has come to us, but skipping back, re-thinking for ourselves and then re-applying the same ideology and philosophy for today's challenges and today's problems.

During these meetings I have found tremendous scope amongst the District Magistrates for us to build on. There is tremendous awareness, there is tremendous integrity and there is tremendous drive. If we can get all these going, all down one road, without too many pulls and pushes, I have no doubt that India can really move ahead to its rightful place, the place we held before we went under, so to say. We were then at the pinnacle. People were, looking for India from across the globe. They would, sail for two years, three years, looking for India. Why? Because India, had the basic philosophy, India had the best technology of the times, India had everything. It had the riches, both intellectual and material. In the couple of hundred years of colonisation, we have fallen behind. India can and must and will get back to that position. For, that, we need this drive, starting at the base, starting at the grassroots. This is really what I feel you must do.

******

Since the achievement of Independence, and more particularly, since the advent of planned development, the country has looked to the district administration to serve as the principal instrument for the country's development. The administration is the vehicle of delivery. Its efficiency determines whether development really reaches the people. It is also the perspectives and approaches of the district administrators which, in many ways, determine the content of development. Whether development concentrates merely on rapid economic growth or extends to social reform, distributive justice and human resource development, depends in good measure on the attitudes of the district administration. That is why it is essential that district administrators relate the details of their daily, tasks to the larger national goals of democracy, socialism, secularism and non-alignment. That is also why it is important that our administrators be imbued with the essential values of our millennial traditions: Truth and Non-violence; tolerance and compassion; one humanity and one world. I have explained in previous inaugural addresses at Bhopal, Hyderabad and Imphal this broader context in which I would like you to consider the specific tasks of evolving a more responsive administration. Those speeches have been circulated to you: Today, I propose to be more pointed and specific.

The major conclusions emerging from the earlier Workshops are, that a truly responsive administration must have two essential characteristics; it must be representative, and it must be responsible.

At present, most district administrations are not representative, because we have allowed democratically elected local bodies do exist, planning and development functions are, to a large extent, divorced from these institutions. A district administration that is not a democratic administration cannot be a representative administration. A major systemic increase in responsiveness will arise out of making district administration more representative.

The other significant systemic reason for the lack of responsiveness in our administration is that there is inadequate devolution of authority and responsibility to the district level. Even such responsibility as has been devolved has become so diffused that no one really knows at which point in the administration responsibility really lies. There is no longer a single focal point in the district administration. No one person feels he or she is responsible. The second major lacuna in our not having a really responsive administration is that we do not have a really responsible administration.

At this Workshop, I would like you to focus your attention on the specific question of how to make district administration: (a) more representative, and (b) more responsible so that we end up with an administration that is altogether more responsive. We do not want snap answers from you. We want you to cogently argue out in writing the pros and cons of all the issues involved. The paper that emerges from this Workshop should be of seminal importance. It should enable us to conduct a really meaningful national debate. We hope to reach reasoned conclusions that enjoy the consensus and support of the country's polity, and bureaucracy as a whole. With a view to facilitating your task in this regard, we have reduced the number of groups into which you will be divided with increased opportunities for interaction among the groups.

A Theme Paper, based on discussions in earlier Workshops, sets out the issues on which we want you to reflect earnestly and deeply. The paper you produce must be detailed and specific. It must be worded with care and enjoy the broad support of the Group and the Workshop as a whole. Where there is disagreement, the alternative views must be set out clearly and cogently.

The first Group will be addressing itself to the question of a democratic framework for district planning. We have had long and varied experience, in different parts of the country, with elections to Panchayati Raj Institutions at the village, mandal and zila levels.

Constitutional provisions have ensured free and fair elections to Parliament and the State Assemblies. While elections to these bodies have been held regularly, elections to local bodies have been sporadic and uncertain. Local bodies have often been superseded. Elected representatives in local bodies have often been replaced by nominated persons. In your view, what measures need to be taken to ensure regular elections to Panchayati Raj Institutions?

Second, how should such elections be supervised? Third, should all Panchayati Raj Institutions be elected directly by the people? Or would there be merit in basing elections to membership or office on some other indirect basis? You might consider this question in the light of the relationship of MPs and MLAs to the work of Zila Parishads, as well as the question of safeguards for the weaker sections.

Group I may then address themselves to another set of

questions relating to the responsibilities of the Panchayati Raj Institutions. What are the subjects which should be assigned to their jurisdiction? Should the devolution of these responsibilities be a matter of administrative discretion or should they be more firmly based?

To ensure that responsibility is not merely a matter of additional powers, should there not be a requirement for local bodies to raise a part of their own revenues? The theme paper refers to the interesting revenue-raising experiments carried out by district planning bodies in Gujarat.

Also within the ambit of responsibilities to be devolved to elected district bodies, I would like you to give consideration to the question of the protection of the rights of the weaker sections. There is the genuine apprehension expressed that dominant interests of caste or community or sheer economic muscle-power, especially in rural areas, will use, or misuse, the electoral process to ride roughshod over the interests of the weaker sections. It has also been pointed out in earlier Workshops that in tribal areas, whatever the electoral standing and electoral representation of the tribal population, the non-tribal minority tends to quickly dominate elected bodies and use them to exploit the tribals. What special safeguards would you recommend?

Group I would also need to look into the relationship between bodies for district planning and development, on the one hand, and full-fledged elected Zila Parishads on the other. Where should the final powers of decision-making be vested?

Finally, Group I should ask itself whether to recommend a single model uniformly applicable to the whole country, or whether it would suggest that the model be modified to take account of special circumstances. With the immense diversity of our country, would you recommend one model with some exceptions? Or a number of fixed models? Or, at the other extreme, leave it to each State, to devise its own model or models?

Group II has the very important task of reflecting upon the relationship between the official administration and elected Panchayati Raj Institutions, the role of each officer in the administration, and his relationship with officers of other services. How will the workload and relationship work with more devolution of powers?

In this light we would like you to thoroughly examine the structure of the official machinery from the district level through the block and tehsil levels, right down to the VLW. In doing this, you must remember that the structure must be capable of providing full official back-up support to the machinery of planning up to and including the district level. It must also, perhaps more importantly, be capable of fulfilling its functions in the implementation of the district plan. When we talk of district planning, responsibility can clearly not be limited to helping formulate the plan. There is much more that needs to be dope in terms of implementation. The structure should also indicate the different disciplines that need to be incorporated to make for effective planning. The theme paper suggests additional disciplines that must be represented in the planning machinery. You should consider the sources from which officers of sufficient experience might be drawn to live and work in the district. You would have to consider what facilities and compensatory allowances might be required to attract officers of sufficient experience. You should also go into the question of utilising local talent, available in local colleges and institutions and various professions, which could be inducted into the planning process. Would this considerably increase the numbers or would it reduce the total numbers in the administrative system? You might also see how to integrate voluntary organisations and co-operative societies into the overall system. There is also the ticklish question to be considered of the role of the MPs and MLAs for the area in the deliberative and decision-making processes of district planning.

The Group should then turn its attention to the integration of this official machinery with the elected bodies. It would not do to have a system where Panchayati Raj Institutions are elected but real power resides elsewhere or with non-elected officials. District planning should be founded on district democracy. What model or models of district administration would you suggest which would fulfil this purpose?

Group II has a complex and difficult task ahead of it. I would expect them to argue their point of view. In detail, take into account different models, and present us with a very detailed organisation chart, or, indeed, several charts, if they come to the conclusion that more than one model is required.

Group III is charged with the nitty-gritty of district planning. To facilitate your comprehension of what needs to go into the exercise, the Planning Commission have arranged for four district planning models, drawn from four different ecological zones, to be presented to you at this Workshop. The District Magistrates of these four districts are here to assist you in understanding the models that have been prepared. By going into the details of these models, you would be able to draw your key lessons of general applicability.

For effective district planning, the first requirement would appear to be as detailed, comprehensive and easily retrievable data as necessary. Not too little; even more important, not too much. This would be the context in which the computer-based DISNIC system would prove its true worth. We must ensure the proper synchronization of computer hardware so that no difficulties arise later on this score.

The second major requirement of effective district planning is a need-based perspective, within a projection of what must be achieved over, say, a five-year or ten-year period, the district planning authorities would be able to prepare a proper annual plan which takes into account the constraints of the resources available. In the absence of a long-term need-based perspective, there would be endless confusion over how to allocate scarce resources amongst competing ends. Allied to this point is the need for district planners to have a thorough familiarity with, and understanding of, national goals and State Government objectives. Clearly what is done at the district level must dovetail into the national plan. You might consider how best this might be ensured.

You should then turn your attention to the question of district budgeting. Too many of the existing district planning bodies tend to confuse budgeting with planning. Yet, district planning, which has to take available resources, and their allocation between different uses as fixed, cannot be particularly meaningful. We have to build feasible financial flexibility into district planning. This is also the appropriate context in which to consider the question of elected district and sub-district authorities raising some part of their own revenues.

District planners will be faced with many of the same difficult choices which confront planning bodies at State and Central levels. Indeed, the choices will be even more acute and painful because the district planner is so much closer to those between whose interests he is required to choose. Planning cannot consist of listing everybody's dreams. Planning is, essentially, a question of choosing a reality from amongst the dreams. It is essential that the resources should not be spread too thinly, in the interest of some kind of paper equality. Since district planning must be based on watersheds, ground water aquifers, soil differences and other variables, there has to be a selective use of resources in identified areas, not a blind mathematical division of resources among different sub-areas.

This also raises the question of the primary unit of planning. Should this be the district or the block? In some States, where district planning has been rather more effective than in others, the block has been taken as the primary unit. You might wish to explore this matter in depth. You might also want to consider what the priority areas for district planning should be. Planning will always have a major Central and State component, implementation of which takes place at the district level.

How are these to be co-ordinated with district plans, both at the planning and the implementation stage? Should district plans concentrate specifically on particular areas such as the Minimum Needs Programmes, the Special Component Plan and the Tribal Sub-plan? How far would one go in giving powers to Zila Parishads, Mandal Panchayats and Gram Sabhas for sanctioning and re-appropriating funds?

Group III should also consider linkages between different development agencies, including co-operatives and banks and other institutions which fall outside the government-run system as such.

I will not say much at this stage about Group IV, which will be consolidating and refining the recommendations made by previous Workshops on a whole series of matters relating to responsive administration but which, strictly speaking, fall outside the purview of district democracy and district planning. I have said much about these matters in my previous inaugural addresses. I have also spent several hours with nearly twenty different Groups which have considered these questions. I would only emphasise that the members of Group IV should attempt to relate these specific concerns to the larger national goals which I have referred to in my addresses at Bhopal, Hyderabad and Imphal.

I have had to resist the temptation to list the questions. I have in mind in too much detail. I have also wanted to leave you as free as possible to come up with your own independent but well-considered conclusions. I look forward to being with you on Monday evening and Tuesday morning to see how we can give meaningful content to our basic equation, namely, that Representativeness and Responsibility equal Responsiveness.

★★★★★★

When we began this series of Workshops on Responsive Administration, our attention was primarily focused on the nitty-gritty of problems at the interface between the district administration and the people the administration is designed to serve. But it soon became clear that the underlying problem was not so much a matter of simplifying procedures or establishing grievance redressal machinery but was fundamentally of a systemic nature. It quickly became apparent that if our district administration is not sufficiently responsive, the basic reason is that it is not sufficiently representative. With the decay of Panchayati Raj Institutions, the administration has got isolated from the people—thus, dulling its sensitivity to the needs of the people.

A consensus also grew that a paternalistic model of district administration is not suitable for a society where the main thrust of administration is on development. It was agreed that the regulatory functions of administration should not be seen as an end in themselves, as they tended to be in colonial times, but as a means of reinforcing and sustaining the processes of broad-based development. There is also general agreement that a more representative and therefore, more responsive administration would be better placed to relate the purposes of district administration to the larger goals of our national life—democracy, socialism, secularism and non-alignment.

At the same time, there is widespread concern at the whittling down of the powers and authority of the District Magistrate without, however, any corresponding whittling down of his responsibilities. In fact, the District Magistrate's responsibilities have increased and diversified in proportion to the diminution of his powers and authority. This has led to indiscipline and confusion in the administration which manifest themselves in various forms of unresponsiveness. It is, therefore, necessary to restore to the District Magistrate his role as the single focal point of the district administration.

This is easier said than done. Some of the District Magistrates we have met at previous Workshops seemed to think that it would be possible to restore the power and authority of the office of District Magistrate by some sort of fiat or decree from the Central or State Government. To think along these lines is to misunderstand the nature of the historical processes at work. The office of District Magistrate has declined in significance and importance because it has not adapted itself to the changing realities. The major reality of post-Independence India is the assertion of the people's will. The position of the District Magistrate can be restored only if it reinforces the democratic process and is responsive to the people. The attempt to preserve the office of District Magistrate as a kind of island of benevolent paternalism rising above the surging waves of democracy is what has resulted in the District Magistrate's island being eroded. The basic task before you is to see how the pristine powers and authority of the office of District Magistrate can be meshed into and harmonized with the processes of democratic decentralization so that the forces of democracy reinforce the prestige and powers of the District Magistrate, even as the prestige and powers of the District

Magistrate are so exercised as to reinforce the processes of democracy.

It has also emerged from the previous Workshops that development which devolves to the district from higher levels tends to be a form of development which is not sufficiently responsive to the needs of the people living in the district. In the absence of district planning, we have planning for projects and planning for programmes but not really planning for the people. Also, planning must encompass much more than government schemes. It must act as a catalyst to involve the people in their own development, so that the people are not merely the passive recipients of the fruits of development but participate actively in the generation of development. That is why I have already announced that the Eighth Plan must be built upwards from the district and not, as in the past, conceived at ethereal levels and filtered down to the district. It is also likely that plans which have been conceived at district level will be more conscientiously implemented at the district level, which is the level at which most of our people interface with the administration. Many of the District Magistrates we have met at previous Workshops have shown themselves enthusiastic about district planning but reserved and cautious about vesting decisions regarding district planning in an elected authority. Other District Magistrates have opined that effective district planning must go hand in hand with Panchayati Raj. Panchayati Raj without district planning might be a somewhat hollow shell, even as district planning without Panchayati Raj would be unrepresentative and, therefore, perhaps less than responsive to the people's felt needs.

Democratic district planning requires expertise. We should not look for this expertise by vastly expanding the size of the administrative machinery. Already, the costs of administration, that is the costs of delivery, are eating up too large a proportion of the resources available. The people benefit from only a small fraction of the total outlay. For making district planning effective, a few additional posts might be required but, by and large, the process must draw upon and develop local talent. Such talent is available in almost all districts in local colleges and other educational institutions, in voluntary agencies operating in the area, in professional organisations and the community at large. Your task here is to see how best to marry the institutions of Panchayati Raj with the requirements of district planning so that without any sacrifice of technical excellence, it becomes possible to produce a district plan which reflects the needs, aspirations and priorities of the people. Even as district planning based on representative political institutions will reflect the people's priorities and aspirations, so will district planning which involves the participation of local, resident expertise better incorporate the interests of the community. Therefore, in studying in detail the four district plans which are before you, I would like you not only to pay attention to their strengths and weaknesses and the lessons they hold, but also consider the mechanisms we must devise to ensure greater expertise and greater local participation in the planning process. Our goal must be excellence without augmenting the costs of administration.

Democratic decentralization is not merely a devolution of power. It must also comprise a devolution of responsibility. There are two major responsibilities which the institutions of democracy must exercise. The first is financial discipline. Authorities who merely spend can never be financially responsible. For fiscal discipline and responsible planning, it is essential that at least some part of revenues and resources be raised by the spending authority. This is indeed a question far larger than the mere balancing of budgets.

Experience has taught us that when the nexus between revenue-earning and expenditure is broken, it becomes tempting to look for populist welfare schemes at the expense of hard development. A proper balance must be maintained. In the ultimate analysis, if the right balance is not maintained, this would be to the detriment of the people. When the community realises that it is itself contributing to the development process, the chances are that the accent will remain on balanced development with long-run advantages rather than only populist short-term measures pursued at the cost of long-term development. It is, therefore, important that you go into this aspect of the issues before you.

The second major responsibility which devolves on Panchayati Raj Institutions is protecting and safeguarding the interests of the weaker sections of society: the Scheduled Castes and Scheduled Tribes, the minorities, women and other disadvantaged or potentially disadvantaged sections of society. The apprehension has been voiced that in so unequal a society as ours, the first consequence of Panchayati Raj will be to reinforce the dominance of the already dominant socio-economic groups. This apprehension needs to be taken into consideration very seriously, is it because elections to Panchayati Raj Institutions are sporadic and uncertain that there is a tendency for these institutions to be dominated by the dominant groups? If so, if we are able to ensure regular periodic elections to these bodies, is the same process likely to operate at the Panchayati Raj level as we have already seen operating in the State Assemblies and Parliament, namely, the dilution of dominance by vested class and caste interests. In the State Assemblies and Parliament, we have seen that dominant socio-economic groups splinter by loyalties to rival political parties and also the need to enter into coalitions of interest with other groups, especially those which might be economically and socially weaken but are numerically stronger. The regular functioning of democracy in Panchayati Raj Institutions will itself ensure, over a period of time, that there is no monopoly of power by dominant socio-economic groups. While this is the long-term solution, in the immediate future there will be serious problems unless we build, constitutional and legislative safeguards into the system from the very beginning. There also has to be specific attention paid to such matters as effective tribal control 'over the expenditure of Tribal Sub-plan funds and effective Scheduled Caste control over the expenditure of Special Component Plan funds. We would like you, to give, the deepest attention to this question of safeguards, checks and balances and the involvement of the weaker sections in Panchayati Raj Institutions to ensure that democratic decentralization is not detrimental to their interests.

In earlier Workshops, there was evidence of two different trends of thought. One is the gradualist approach, which would wish to see a phased replacement of a bureaucratic administration by full-fledged democratic district administration. The other is that we must take the plunge now, and unreservedly base responsive administration upon representative administration. We would want you to flesh out the arguments for and against these two views, which have, so far, been set out only in somewhat skeleton form. The consensus you build on this will crucially determine your views on all that follows: the structure of Panchayati Raj Institutions, the responsibilities to be devolved through democratic decentralization, the relationship between district officialdom and the elected authority the content and methodology of district planning. Therefore, I would like you to go through in detail the alternatives of the gradualist approach *versus* the direct approach.

Related to this is the question of the pace at which democratic decentralization must reach below the Zila Parishad level to mandal Panchayats and Gram Sabhas. Should decentralization to these levels be simultaneous with the introduction of district-level democracy or would it be better to consolidate democratic institutions at the district level before going down to lower levels? We also seek your views on whether the President of the Zila Parishad should be elected directly by the people or by an electoral college comprising the members of the Zila Parishad and possibly, subordinate elected bodies. Please also deliberate upon the need or otherwise to have a District Planning Board separate from the Zila Parishad. Would the needs of responsive district administration be best met by Zila Parishad which is akin to a form of district government or would it be better to have a multiplicity of bodies with separate jurisdictions? And if the central role in district planning is assigned to the Zila Parishad, how do we associate other elected representatives, like MPs, MLAs and MLCs with the exercise?

In previous Workshops, considerable attention has been paid to matters of administrative detail. We have a host of recommendations regarding personnel matters, service conditions and transfers. We also have recommendations regarding the simplification of procedures, grievance redressal and innovations in district administration. We have been told that the cutting edge of the administration is not really the District Magistrate but lies much lower, at the block and village level. I have suggested that we might regard the cutting edge as being like a modern razor, with several successive cutting edges! The problems of personnel, motivation and training at these levels have been highlighted and interesting suggestions offered. Particular mention has been made of the problems arising from the complete separation of the judiciary from the executive, as also the relationship between the Police Service and the Civil Service. What X would like you to do at this Workshop is to integrate these disparate suggestions into a unified view of how to make district administration more responsive by making it more representative. For example, at Jaipur, somebody came out with a proposal for establishing a Board to exercise general control and supervision over the grievance redressal machinery. Should there be a separate Board or should this become an essential function of an elected Zila Parishad?

The different issues on which we seek your views have been set out with considerable competence in the theme paper which is before you as well as the summaries of points arising out of the deliberations of previous Workshops on the different sub-themes. I would like to congratulate Minister Chidambaram and his colleagues on the excellent work they have done in preparing these papers. At this final Workshop, I would like the different Groups to study and elaborate the summaries of each of the sub-themes rather than start the exercise *de novo*. Some of the arguments have been somewhat hastily or sketchily set out. There are some points which have, perhaps, not been taken into consideration. One would, of course, encourage you to provide any new ideas you might have on the different subjects. So, each of the Groups should build upon the paper that already exists, but without regarding the points mentioned in the papers as any kind of constraint on their own freedom of thought and action.

We have found in the past that some District Magistrates

tend to feel under an obligation to defend the model they are familiar with rather than exercise their own independence of judgement. We would like you to feel quite unfettered by your previous experience or the present practice. We are interested in what you think is the best model, not necessarily the model which you are presently administering. If you think conditions obtaining in different parts of the country warrant several different models, please set out in detail the alternatives you would suggest. However, it is important to ensure that the different models you suggest do not represent different degrees of democratic decentralization. Clearly the representativeness of Panchayati Raj Institutions must be approximately the same everywhere in the country even if the particular form or structure is varied to meet local requirements.

I also hope there will be much more and better co-ordination among the Groups at Coimbatore than was in evidence at some earlier Workshops. Such co-ordination can only come about through greater interaction between the Groups. When reports are prepared within each Group without reference to the reports being prepared by other Groups, anomalies are felt unresolved. I hope you will be able to so organise your work that Group reports are discussed in a plenary session among yourselves before we get down to any discussions with each of the Groups on Monday evening and Tuesday morning.

I hope the discussions at the Coimbatore Workshop will be marked by sparkle and zest. You would have heard from your colleagues who attended the previous Workshops that we encourage the exchange of experience, that we welcome bold and innovative thinking, and that we discourage anyone being inhibited by his present position in the administrative hierarchy. You represent the intellectual elite of the country. You are part of the administrative system that, almost uniquely among developing countries, has given independent India continuity and stability. Your colleagues in previous Workshops have demonstrated a remarkable commitment to the basic themes of our modern nationhood—democracy, socialism, secularism and non-alignment. They have also shown themselves to be dedicated, hardworking and upright. I have no doubt that you share these characteristics with your colleagues. It only increases your responsibility to furnish us with cogent, consistent proposals for making our district administration more representative, more responsible and, therefore, more responsive.

4

Focus on Panchayati Raj

I am happy to attend this *Sammelan*. First, I wish to thank the Ministry for choosing such an appropriate day for this *Sammelan* which falls between our 40th Republic Day and the anniversary of the martyrdom of Gandhiji. When we adopted our Constitution on the first Republic Day, we promised to give power to the people. Gandhiji fought against the British, the imperialist forces, for achieving this object. I am particularly happy that we have got an opportunity to discuss this seriously during the next two days. I have a complaint which I wanted to make in the end, but I am making at the outset. Bhajan Lalji has invited eight thousand people to come to Delhi but he has fixed only two days and one night for discussions. I am told that the entire time will be utilised if only two per cent of the invitees speak for five minutes each. I feel that in such a short duration we cannot discuss these matters well. I hope Bhajan Lalji will extend the *Sammelan* by another two days, to enable at least double the number of speakers to express their views. I hope he will do so and will also extend the arrangements in the camp.

After Independence, we had promised in the Constitution, to strengthen the third level of our democracy. The first and the second levels which are governed from Delhi and the State capitals, have been strengthened following several elections, and no one can weaken them. The third level, however, is weak and it affects the first two levels also, because people at the top level have become paper tigers and the structure has become hollow. This has to be set right by strengthening the Panchayati

Raj Institutions. To strengthen our democracy in Delhi and in the State capitals, it is essential to strengthen the democratic Institutions at the Panchayat level. To gear up the development process, it is necessary to strengthen the Panchayati Raj Institutions at district, block and village levels.

In the last one-and-a-half year, we have done many things in this context. We began by organising discussions with the District Magistrates and Collectors. We talked to the Secretaries and the Chief Secretaries. There were discussions in our Party and in the Ministries. We have come to you after doing our home work. I hope we will help you and fulfil the promises we had made. Promises were made during the freedom struggle and in our Constitution but no one effectively implemented them. The people at the top level were busy strengthening their own positions in politics as well as in administration and completely neglected the federal institutions. Whenever elections to the Panchayats were held, they remained nominal. And for the last 10-20 years, mostly nominated members are running these institutions (Panchayats). This cannot strengthen the base level. The devolution of power to the grassroots level as promised could not be affected and whatever was done was generally in an arbitrary manner. In some States where devolution of power had been implemented a member was nominated to the local bodies by the administration or a Minister was placed there. What actually happened? The decision-making authority remained either with the State Government or with the administration, and it could not filter down to the base level.

In addition, sufficient resources were not made available for the upliftment of the rural population, and the meagre amount provided was not spent according to the needs of the rural people. In our development planning and implementation, the participation of the Panchayati Raj Institutions was lacking. What was the net result? The result was that the power, which Gandhiji and Panditji wanted to be given to the people and for which our Constitution also provided, did not actually reach them. It meant that the plans and the schemes made, could not in reality cater to your needs. The development programmes which were worked out from Delhi and the State capitals could neither improve your conditions nor remove your difficulties. The result was that even after the completion of those schemes, their full benefit could not reach you.

Whatever economic development was achieved could not be effective because there was a vast gap between the preparation of the schemes and their implementation. The result was that even for the solution of trifling issues, the people looked to the Government. I can quote the example of my own constituency which I have known minutely as to how people come to me even with small problems. There must be some lacuna somewhere that MPs, MLAs and even Chief Ministers come to me with trifling matters. Those issues which can be tackled at the village level should be dealt with there. If the Central Government is involved in such issues, what requires to be done can neither be done well nor in time. You know, there are many procedural requirements in the implementation of a project which involves many people, and these only create problems. When we attempt rural development from Delhi, we are unable to detect all the loopholes which only you can plug, being on the spot. The result is that you come with complaints that development schemes are not being properly implemented.

We must ensure that our people are not totally dependent on the Central Government or the State Governments for all types of development works. They should themselves have a feeling of participation in development programmes and the process of social change. This will require that the gap between the administration and the people be bridged. We have to see that people, whether they are in politics or in Government, should not rush to Delhi or State capitals for the redressal of every grievance. If development work can be planned at the district, block or village level it should be taken up there itself. If this is not done, schemes will be delayed and so will their implementation.

We wanted to remove social injustice and atrocities on the weaker sections but this task has not yet been completed. Even today atrocities are perpetrated on weaker sections, on Scheduled Castes and Scheduled Tribes and on women. We want to involve people in nation building. We want everyone in the country to take initiative in such work. This, however, has not been fully accomplished and the result is that a system of power-brokers has emerged in our country, whether it is politics or the development process. For any work that is to be done, people have to please some power-broker. We have to break this system and to do this, we have to devolve maximum power to Panchayati Raj Institutions. This was the desire of Gandhiji and Panditji. But that spirit got lost on the way. We will, however, try to give you strength on the lines Gandhiji and Panditji wanted.

It is essential to give power to the common people. We have to pay special attention to the weaker sections, the Scheduled Castes, the Scheduled Tribes and women. We have also to take special care of linguistic and other minorities and protect them. We have also to keep a watch so that devolution of power to grassroots is not usurped by the rich and those who derive power from the caste structure. The Panchayati Raj System should ensure social justice to the poor, to the weaker sections. I would like to have your suggestions on these issues.

I want you to speak openly on these issues during the four days of the *Sammelan*. But you should remember that whatever system of devolution of power is evolved, it must ensure protection of the weak. The elections should be held in time and the weaker sections should freely participate in the elections. If need be, some sort of reservation could be evolved. You have to think how to fill the reserved seats or posts. Should these be filled by election or by nomination? Should we follow the procedure adopted in some countries where the candidate defeated with the minimum margin is also declared elected? Or should we adopt some other method? Every system has its own strong points.

There are various systems—each with its own weakness and strength. You have to consider these systems from different angles.

You have to pay special attention to the weaker sections and tell me how they can be helped. Another method can be what was, at one time in vogue for elections to the Lok Sabha, the system of multi-member constituencies. Yet another method could also be one of setting up social justice committees and special committees in areas inhabited by *Harijans, Adivasis,* minorities and other weaker sections.

You have to discuss seriously and evolve some kind of a relationship between Panchayati Raj Institutions and the State Governments. You have to discuss it minutely because any mistake can stop the development process. You have to ponder over the relationship of Collectors and District Magistrates with Zila Parishads and their Chairmen. Again, you have to think which institutions would function under the Zila Parishad, under the block and at village level.

You must discuss how development schemes can be implemented most effectively. You should not be engaged in creating small kingdoms because these will only further weaken us. The relationship of municipal areas with Zila Parishads is an important factor, whether they should maintain equal status with Zila Parishads or work within them or under them. Each system has its own strength and weakness. If a district government is formed, it will strengthen the Zila Parishad. Small towns within such a set-up will become focal points of development. On the other hand if Zila Parishads are kept outside the district administration it will focus greater attention on the development of rural areas. Both the systems are relevant in their own way. You have to find out a way so that a balance can be maintained. Today it is not sufficient only to plan for the development of rural areas. Educated youth are looking for a different type of employment and better facilities for which they migrate to small towns and cities. You must evolve a framework that draws upon the strengths of the alternative systems. You must evolve a system which accelerates the work of removing poverty. You must discuss what role can be played at the district, block and village levels in the planning process.

I have asked the Planning Commission to formulate plans from the district level for the Eighth Plan. They have assured that a beginning will be made. Constraints of time may not permit us to make a beginning on the scale we had envisaged but we will find a way out. I hope that by the second or third year of the Eighth Plan, this work will get off the ground well and that there will be co-ordination between the State Planning bodies and the Planning Commission.

Then, there is the major problem of resources. You must ensure proper utilisation of resources. I feel that if we keep on giving resources as we are doing today, that will not lead to proper development. You will keep on asking for funds and nobody will see whether work is being carried out properly or not. For the most part you do not keep in view your actual requirements when funds are made available from very far away and programmes are also made at some distant place. You have your eye on what is surplus with the Government and what you can get from it. The other point is that these funds are not linked with raising resources. That is why you must find out whether at the district and lower levels some resources can be raised. Whether you can be given some powers to raise revenue and in what way could these be given.

You will also have to discuss how power will be devolved. When the Panchayati Raj System was initiated, the responsibility of giving power to local bodies was with the States. Often power given by one hand was taken away by the other. This should not happen again. How should the power be given to you? Straight from the Centre or from the States to the local bodies? No one should be able to take this power away from you. Should the Constitution be amended and in what manner and to what extent? What is the minimum amendment required and what is the maximum that should be done? At the very minimum, timely elections to Panchayats must be ensured and these bodies should not be dissolved without valid reasons. If for some reason they are dissolved, there should be a provision for their re-election as is the case for our Lok Sabha or State Assemblies. This is the minimum requirement. There can also be much more. You must reflect which is the best middle path and how we can reach it. We do not want to give you Panchayati Raj Institutions as they were. We want to renew and strengthen the institutions that we give you, so that elections are held in time and real power is in your hands. We have also to learn from the past 25 years of experience, what we could achieve and what we could not, where the weakness lies and how it can be remedied.

Responsibilities should be well defined and resources should be properly allocated to you. Above all we must ensure that weaker sections are protected and that they are not weakened by this system but in fact gain strength from it.

I hope this new system will cater to the actual needs of the people. It must ensure that past mistakes are not repeated. I hope that democracy will reach the grassroots. To achieve this object, we have to break the hold of power-brokers and give real power to the districts, blocks and villages to the people who live there.

Even a four-day period for such discussions is not sufficient and therefore, a questionnaire has been given to you. I hope you will study the questionnaire seriously, complete it and return it to us. I assure you that we will go through the questionnaires filled up by you, thoroughly and try to incorporate your suggestions.

I hope that I shall be with you again on the fourth day and for a longer period. I have kept two and a half hours apart to be with you. I have spoken a lot today, but on that day I will speak less and listen more to you. And I hope that you will speak openly without any reservation.

I see that only a few women are present here. I hope Bhajan Lalji will see to it that women delegates get full opportunity for expressing their views.

In the end, I welcome you to Delhi, and I hope that the arrangement made for your stay here is comfortable, in spite of the chilly weather. If there are any shortcomings, do please let us know and we will try our best to remove these. I saw you sitting in two blocks yesterday in the Republic Day function. I am sure you must have enjoyed the parade.

It is appropriate that you visited the *Samadhi* of Gandhiji before beginning your deliberations. You have before you very significant work—work linked with the thoughts and ideals of Gandhiji and an integral part of our freedom struggle, which in a way was left out and must be completed now. I give you my good wishes for the success of your discussions. When I meet you on the fourth day of the *Sammelan*, I hope to get from you good and solid answers to the questions which I have posed before you.

5

People's Participation in Planning Process

I am very happy that the Planning Commission has taken the initiative to organise this Conference on the Indian Planning. Experience as part of the celebrations of the 40th anniversary of Independence and the Jawaharlal Nehru Centenary.

Jawaharlal Nehru was the visionary who first conceived and conceptualised the role of planning in the post-independence task of nation-building. He was the architect who built the institutions of planning. He was the statesman who gave these institutions a major role in policy-making. To him, planning was not a matter of dogma or ideology, nor of mere technical or economic management. He saw planned development as the instrument for social and economic uplift, of our people, for transforming and modernising our society. He saw planning as the means of building a strong economy which, would safeguard our national independence and enable India to take her rightful place in the world. His vision is as relevant today as it was then.

The planning process has made a significant contribution to the structural transformation of the Indian economy. There are gaps, some of them crucial, but today, we can look at ourselves with a degree of confidence and hope as we move forward to realise the India we all want:

- an India free of poverty, providing social justice and equality of opportunity for all its citizens;

- a society in social harmony, with a pattern of individual and social life which blends modernity with our traditional values;
- an economy which is strong, self-reliant and at the frontiers of technology;
- a country committed to peace and international co-operation.

This Conference is especially well-timed as we are nearing the end of the Seventh Plan period and work has already begun on formulating the Eighth Plan. It is, therefore, an appropriate time to look back on what we have achieved and learnt from the experience even as we set new goals and devise new strategies for the future. Planning is ultimately a practical and not a theoretical exercise. To be effective it must be firmly based on a critical appreciation of our strengths and weaknesses so that we can reinforce the one and correct the other.

The Conference is also timely because there is an intellectual ferment in many countries including most of the socialist world on planning and planning methods. In all these countries, there is extensive reappraisal and examination of traditional methods of planning and control. There is an active search for new methods of management and a great desire to experiment. Some of the problems faced by these countries are not very different from our own. There may be lessons to be learnt from both their past experiences and their ongoing experiments.

This Conference has brought together a large number of distinguished individuals, who have been directly involved in the planning in the past. I am sure the wisdom and wealth of experience of such a gathering will provide valuable guidance to the Commission as it moves towards formulating the Eighth Plan. I would like to take this opportunity to share my thoughts on the broad features of our economic situation today, as also to raise some issues which I think will need priority attention as we plan for the future.

First, I would like to mention some positive developments. Our recent economic performance has been good and gives good reason for satisfaction. The growth rate at the economy, which was earlier locked at around 3.5 to 4 per cent has clearly accelerated to a level of around 5 per cent or so. This was evident on the basis of the Sixth Plan performance. It has been amply endorsed by the experience of the first four years of the Seventh Plan.

Although there was poor rainfall in first two years of the Seventh Plan and the third was a year of severe drought, the situation was well managed. The momentum of development was not disturbed. Agriculture performed better than in previous drought years while industrial growth continued at a high rate. With good rains in the current year, the economy has responded with vigorous growth. Foodgrains production will exceed the target of 166 million tonnes and may reach an impressive record level of 170 million tonnes. Industrial production is growing at over 9 per cent per year. GDP growth is expected to be around 10 per cent. This will take the average growth rate of the economy in the first four years of the Seventh Plan to around 5.5 per cent compared with the 5 per cent target for the full five year period.

Apart from the overall growth rate, there are definite signs of improved performance in certain areas which are critical for the future performance of the economy. One of these is infrastructure which is a critical determinant of the potential growth of the economy. It is also wholly in the public sector and its functioning is, therefore, a special responsibility of the Government. All the major infrastructure sectors have shown good performance in the Seventh Plan. Production growth in these sectors has been on target. Large investments have been made, adding to capacity. Much needed modernisation has been brought about in key areas. Railways and power have shown notable improvements in productivity indices. This suggests an improvement in efficiency and management which augurs well for the future.

Another area where performance in the Seventh Plan has been very good relates to project management in the public sector. All the major fertilizer projects taken up for implementation in the public sector and co-operative sector, such as the giant Maharashtra Gas Cracker Complex and

NALCO project, either have been or will be commissioned on schedule within the Seventh Plan period. Improved project management in the public sector and greater efficiency in utilising capacity already created will go a long way towards strengthening our economic performance in the years ahead.

The industrial sector generally has responded well to Government's policy initiative to reduce the degree of regulation and detailed licensing control over investment and production. Indian industry has been encouraged to upgrade technology, modernise and expand. Domestic competition has been substantially increased with favourable effects upon costs and quality. A substantial part of the resources needed for investment has been mobilised from the capital market which has grown in strength.

These developments provide grounds for optimism about the future growth potential of the economy. Therefore, the Planning Commission has been asked to prepare an Approach to the Eighth Plan based on accelerating the growth rate to 6 per cent. This is not an impossible target. But it will not be easy to achieve unless we take care of some of the weaknesses which are evident in our planning experience.

First, I believe the planning process has lost some of the plan it had States face enormous demands in the years ahead to provide resources for expanded programmes in essential areas such as social and economic infrastructure, agriculture and irrigation, anti-poverty programmes and also human resource development. These demands will be even larger if growth is to be accelerated.

We can and should do more to raise additional tax resources. But the scope in this area is limited. The total tax revenue as a percentage of GDP is already quite high. It can be increased further through fiscal reform, widening of the tax base and improved administration. But the larger part of the solution must come from a curtailment of wasteful expenditure and better financial performance by public sector enterprises.

This will pose difficult decisions in the years ahead. Government programmes will have to be operated on much tighter budgets to ensure maximum real benefit per rupee of expenditure. We will have to resort to zero based budgeting or some similar technique to ensure that redundancy is minimised in all programmes and departments. Subsidies will have to be controlled through much tighter targeting to ensure that subsidies go only to those who need them. Systems of autonomy and accountability will have to be introduced in public sector enterprises designed to strengthen the management of these enterprises and improve their financial performance. Wages will have to bear a closer relation to productivity than has been the case in the past.

These steps will not be easy. But they have to be taken in the interest of plan objectives. We have to recognise that strict financial discipline, combined with public sector efficiency, is the only guarantee of being able to finance a large volume of development expenditure without risking inflation.

Although we have made progress in poverty alleviation, the problem remains large and urgent. Part of the solution lies in improving our programmes for small and marginal farmers, especially in areas of low productivity. This is something we have to do in any case to maximise agricultural production. There is disturbing evidence that the rapid growth in our industrial sector in recent years has not been accompanied by a commensurate growth in employment. Employment growth in the organised industrial sector has been especially disappointing.

With our continually growing labour force, a large number of new job seekers enter the labour market each year. We must pay much greater attention in the Eighth Plan to the generation of employment. The bulk of the new jobs must come from employment generated by expansion in the productive sectors of the economy. Much of this will have to be in agriculture where there is at present considerable underemployment. Agro-processing and other agriculture related activities need to be encouraged on a priority basis for this purpose. We must also explore to the full the scope for creating productive non-agricultural jobs in the rural areas. This will ease the pressures for urban migration which would otherwise pose serious problems.

Despite these steps there will remain for some time a residual requirement for employment in rural areas. This will have to be met by special employment programmes. These programmes have been greatly expanded in the Seventh Plan. Proposals to strengthen them further are under consideration.

We will also have to take a hard look at the scope for expanding the employment potential of industry and allied services. The answer does not lie in a blanket encouragement of over manning or in fighting the injection of new technology into industry for fear that it will displace jobs. Such approaches are economically unsustainable and can impose heavy costs, even in terms of the growth of employment itself. At the same time, it must be ensured that economically efficient labour intensive sectors of industry are not placed at a disadvantage compared with highly capital intensive sectors. Industrial planning and fiscal policy will have to pay more attention to these issues.

We also need to recognise the potential for productive job creation in the services sector. This is a large sector in the economy. It is growing rapidly. It has the potential to provide very large opportunities of employment, and self-employment, for the unemployed and the underemployed labour force.

Another area in which we will have to think radically, differently from the way we have done in the past relates to the interface between our economy and the global economy. Thus far we have tended to insulate ourselves from world markets, probably more than most other countries. In recent years, we have deliberately increased the pressure of domestic competition in the economy. But the exposure to foreign competition has not been much increased and for good reasons. As we move into the Eighth Plan and beyond, we must plan for a greater opening up of the economy to the world, allowing far greater exposure to foreign competition through imports. This transition is necessary if we want to modernise and to be internationally competitive. Indian industry can make the transition in a planned and orderly fashion. We have to recognise, however, that the management of the balance of payments will pose major challenges in this process.

The world economic environment is not one which encourages any expectations of easy availability of confessional finance. We can finance a reasonable deficit on the balance of payments through available confessional resources supplemented prudent commercial borrowing. But for the rest, the pace at which we can open up the economy and increase our import absorption, depends crucially upon our ability to export. This is the real measure of self-reliance. True self-reliance does not mean self-sufficiency in all areas. It means the ability to pay through our own export effort for the imports we need.

Export performance is an area which we have tended to neglect. In the Sixth Plan, we achieved only about half the target growth rate of exports in volume terms. The experience in the Seventh Plan has been much better especially in the past two years. But we are still far from having a broad-based export capability. Large parts of our industry remain firmly facing inwards, making little or no effort to export. Industry needs imports of technology, capital goods and materials if it is to modernise. But it must also pay for these imports through much better export performance. Our industrial planning should give to priority to achieving this export capability.

Planning in India has tended to become an increasingly technical exercise. It must remain essentially a political process. It is part of the large exercise of nation-building. We need peace on our frontiers, peace in our region and peace in the world to be able to concentrate resources and attention on issues of economic development and social progress. The country also needs to be at peace with itself. Insurgency, agitations, communal disorder and any disturbance of law and order are all disruptive of the growth process. It is also important that there be a degree of national consensus about the objectives which the nation sets itself and the processes by which these are to be achieved.

Planning should not mean that the Government does everything itself or that the people expect the Government to do everything for them. One function of planning is for Government to directly involve itself in development. The other, and equally important function, is for planning to act as the catalyst to stimulate creativity and enterprise, private and co-operative endeavour. Planning must never become an obstacle to individual and community initiative. We have also tended in recent years to neglect the longer perspective in planning. The nation must not only set itself but also be generally familiar with its own long-term goals and objectives. We must determine the earliest possible date by which it would be feasible to eliminate poverty as defined at present.

We must work towards targets of employment generation that make it realistic to expect a tangible solution within as reasonably short a time as possible. We must know how we intend to phase our priorities over time. We must know what sacrifices and what choices we have to make and when. This would imbue the nation with a sense of purpose and direction. Within such a perspective, life and substance would be given to the cold numbers and percentages of incremental growth rates. It is to these great tasks that our planning experts, our people and the nation as a whole are summoned.

6

Democracy and Development at Doorstep

Thank you for accepting my invitation to attend this Conference. I am aware that many of you have had to postpone important engagements in your State capitals in order to be present here, I am sorry for the inconvenience this might have caused you. I am grateful to you for having taken the trouble to join us on this historic occasion. I use the word "historic" advisedly.

Speech at the Conference of Chief Ministers on Panchayati Raj, New Delhi, 5 May 1989

The struggle for Panchayati Raj was an integral element of our struggle for freedom. Mahatma Gandhi said: "Real *Swaraj* will come not by the acquisition of authority by a few but by the acquisition of the capacity by all."

We fought for freedom so that the people of India might be liberated. Inherent in that liberation was the establishment of democracy as the framework of our political life. Gandhiji taught us that: "True democracy cannot be worked by twenty men sitting at the Centre. It has to be worked from below by the people of every village."

Democracy in our Parliament is deeply entrenched in our Constitution. Democracy in our State Legislatures is sanctified by our Constitution. However, democracy in our Panchayats was left to our good sense to carry out as a Directive Principle of State Policy. Article 12 of the Constitution defines "the State" as including both: "the Government and Parliament of India and the Government and the Legislature of each of the States..."

Article 40 of the Constitution states: "The State shall take steps to organize village Panchayats and endow them with such powers and authority as may be necessary to enable them to function as units of self-government."

Thus, the Centre and the States share the responsibility for bringing Panchayati Raj to fruition. The Constitutional framework for Panchayati Raj is primarily the responsibility of the Centre. The legislative details fall in the province of the States. When we look back on thirty years of country-wide experience of Panchayati Raj, the picture that emerges is not one of the fulfilment of this Directive Principle of State Policy, but one of experiments, some more successful, some less, of experiments persisted with and experiments abandoned, of lessons learned and lessons unlearned, of a diversity of experience, some of which call for recognition and some for national transmission.

I am persuaded that now is the time for us to take stock of the experience of the last thirty years and launch a fresh initiative. I think, I owe it to you to explain why I am of the view that the present is the opportune conjunçture to launch this initiative. I take as my starting point the revision in 1986 of the 29-Point Programme. We laid particular stress on the need to have a responsive administration. I was intrigued by the conundrum that while our Civil Services were taking in some of the finest brains and best administrative ability of the country, highly motivated and deeply dedicated, the experience of the vast majority of our people at the grassroots has been that, at the interface between the people and the administration, the administration is unresponsive, inefficient, unsympathetic, often callous, sometimes even cruel to those whom they are meant to serve. Clearly, this is not a failure of personnel because our personnel are so carefully chosen and so well trained as to be among the best anywhere in the world. It is due to a systemic failure. I thought I would explore this systemic failure with the talented young men and women to whom we have entrusted the administration of our country at the district level and below.

Accordingly, the Union Department of Personnel organized a series of Workshops with District Magistrates, Deputy Commissioners and Collectors on the subject of Responsive Administration. I participated in these Workshops to gain an understanding of what the problem was from the perspective of the persons we have put in-charge of administering our districts. I also wanted to know what they thought, might be the solution. The outlines of an answer began emerging remarkably quickly. Many of the participants in the first Workshop itself stressed that, despite all the goodwill in the world, all their sincerity and all their dedication, a bureaucratic administration, could not be responsive until it was rooted in a democratic polity. The major lesson to be learnt is that a responsive administration has to be a representative administration, an administration which is responsible to the people.

I found in what they said, an echo of the rationale that Jawaharlal Nehru had explained when he launched Panchayati Raj at Nagaur in Rajasthan on Gandhi Jayanti in 1959. He said: "To uplift lakhs of villages is not an ordinary task... The reason for the slow progress is our dependence on official machinery. An officer is probably necessary because he is an expert. But this work can be done only if the people take up the responsibility in their own hands... The people are not merely to be consulted. Effective power has to be entrusted to them."

Based on this penetrating perception which, as I said, became evident even in the first Workshop, I explored with the district officers—what had gone wrong with the experiment launched with such high hopes thirty years ago. I plied them with questions to set their minds thinking. The answers given to us provided the basis for our taking the consultative process to other levels.

The conclusions of the district officers were presented to a Conference of Chief Secretaries convened expressly for this purpose. We also sought the views of Secretaries to the Government of India, many of whom had been district officers at the commencement of Panchayati Raj and, as such, witnessed the rise and fall of Panchayati Raj Institutions, the decline, decay and desuetude of these institutions, as well as their aspirations and achievements.

From there, we carried the consultative process to the political level. A Sub-Committee of the Parliamentary Consultative Committee on Personnel studied the issues over several months and submitted to us a detailed report. The Congress Parliamentary Party shared with us their views. The All-India Congress Committee conducted a series of debates and seminars within Party forums all over the country.

On Republic Day, 1989, we invited to Delhi nearly 8,000 representatives of Panchayati Raj Institutions from the States of northern and western India. These regional consultations were carried forward to the north-eastern and eastern States in Calcutta and the southern States in Bangalore. I would like to place on record our deep appreciation of the co-operation extended to us by the Government of West Bengal and the Government of Karnataka in conducting these regional conferences.

The Union Minister of Agriculture met with Panchayati Raj Ministers from the States at a Conference held, not without significance, in the State capital which draws its name from the Father of the Nation and the Father of Panchayati Raj, Mahatma Gandhi.

It had become evident at an early stage of our deliberations that the weaker sections of our society, specifically the Scheduled Castes, the Scheduled Tribes and women, were grossly under-represented in Panchayati Raj Institutions, inadequate attention was given to their problems, and they did not enjoy an equitable share of the benefits of Panchayati Raj. Therefore, under the aegis of the National Commission for the Scheduled Castes and the Scheduled Tribes, All-India Conferences of Scheduled Caste and Scheduled Tribe Panchayati Raj representatives were held in Delhi. I had the privilege of spending several hours with these representatives. Rarely have I had a more instructive experience, as the poet Robert Burns has said:

"Oh! wad some god
The giftie gi'e us
To see ourselves
As ithers see us."

We have also consulted nearly 800 women representatives of Panchayati Raj Institutions drawn from all over the country.

We come to you, the Chief Ministers of India, in whom is vested the primary responsibility for Panchayati Raj, at the culmination of a consultative process which is without precedent in the annals of Independent India. Never before has a Government at the highest level taken so carefully into account the views of so many tens of thousands of people at every level about democracy and development to be at the grassroots. The proposals we place before you are not really our proposals. They are the proposals of the people of India, articulated through their representatives in Panchayati Raj Institutions. This, in itself, makes this occasion historic.

Democracy without Panchayati Raj is a negation of Mahatma Gandhi's dreams. Development without Panchayati Raj is a negation of Jawaharlal Nehru's vision:

"Real change" said Panditji, "comes, of course, from within the village, from the very people living in the village, and is not imposed from outside."

It is a process of self-development and self-reliance. The transfer of authority for development work to the Panchayats is likely to change the whole background in our rural areas and make the people there more self-reliant and conscious of their responsibilities. In a slightly lighter, vein, Panditji referred to Lenin's famous statement that "Communism is Soviets plus Electricity" and said that, for India, "Progress is Panchayats plus Electric Power"!

How far we have strayed from that vision! Planning in India has become increasingly centralised, not decentralised. It is in Yojana Bhavan and the State Planning Commissions that assessments are made of what the people need and *ex-parte* judgements are given of what the people want and what is good for them. Planning has been transmogrified into a highly technical exercise where complicated equations are balanced and every variable taken into account—except the poor beneficiary of the process! We seem to have forgotten that planning is about people, that planning is for the people, that planning must be undertaken with the people. It is only when planning is based upon the perceptions and propositions of the Panchayati Raj Institutions that it will begin to respond to the felt needs of our populace, to their perspectives, to their aspirations, to their wants, and to their requirements. I want the Eighth Plan to be a humane plan, a Plan built upon the will of the people as articulated by them in forums to which they have ready access.

Even as the drafting of our Plans suffers from the vast chasm that separates the capitals from the places where the Plans are implemented, so does the implementation of our Plans suffer the consequences of the chasm separating the place from where orders are issued and the villages, blocks and districts where these orders are carried out. Because of this vast chasm, the monitoring of implementation has degenerated into the elaboration of statistical tables furnished by the very officers whose work is supposed to be monitored, with little or no two-way communication between those responsible in the field and those who sit in far-away air-conditioned cubby holes. There is only one group which really knows what is happening at the grassroots. They are the people who live at the grassroots. It is to them and their representatives that execution and supervision must be entrusted if such execution and supervision is to have any real effect, any real meaning. Devolution, to be meaningful, has to be a devolution of powers and responsibilities matched by a devolution of finances. Much State legislation deals with these matters. Equally, it is indisputable that the history of Panchayati Raj in India is littered with examples of legislative authority not being translated into administrative reality, of powers devolved being arbitrarily withdrawn, of real authority being transferred from Panchayati Raj Institutions to institutions outside the Panchayati Raj System, and under the control, not of the people, but of the representatives of an outside authority.

The inadequate and uncertain devolution of powers, responsibilities and finances has meant that, in much of India, the people see the administration, not as the servant of their representatives but as a form of bureaucratic dictatorship. Sometimes this dictatorship is benevolent, but at all times unrepresentative. There is no way our administration can be made responsive unless it is made both representative and responsible.

Our administration is also plagued with enormous wastage. The costs of administration eat up a disproportionately high share of the total outlay for schemes and programmes. Leakages of various other kinds occur. The people watch on helplessly as their representatives have little say, and no control, over what is happening. To the proposition that a responsive administration can only be a representative administration, I would add the other proposition that an efficient administration can only be a representative administration.

This is the second reason for which I consider the present juncture as crucial for the launching of new initiative. The people's expectations have risen dramatically. They are not content to acquiesce in their lot. They demand, and rightly so, that we give them opportunity and openings. But, because the responsibility for development does not lie in their hands, their expectation is from the development process, are not linked to an appreciative and awareness of the constraints of resources, the hard choices to be made, and the hard work to be undertaken. We have in Hindi the very expressive phrase: *Mai-baap sarkar*. Since we have reduced the people to recipients of the development process, instead of being participants in the development process, there is a growing rift between what the people demand and what is possible to achieve.

This growing rift has the most dangerous implications for the future of our polity, for the future of our democracy, for the future of our unity and independence. The people have to become part of the development process. This can be done only if representative Panchayati Raj Institutions become the primary instrument for the preparation of Plans and the implementation of the development process.

The experience of thirty years of democracy and development at the grassroots has varied enormously from State to State. There is no State where the experiment has not been tried, either through Panchayati Raj Institutions or through traditional bodies. Equally, there is no State which can claim to have reached perfection in running the institutions of Panchayati Raj. Yet, there has been little cross-fertilisation or interaction between the Panchayati Raj Systems of different States. There has been a tendency to hermetically seal off one Panchayati Raj System from another. The series of regional Panchayati Raj *Sammelans* which we have held is probably the first organised attempt in 30 years of Panchayati Raj to give its representatives the opportunity to get to know each other, to learn from each other, and to benefit as much from each other's successes as from each other's failures.

I am glad and grateful that some Chief Ministers who initially had reservations about this process have now themselves come to this Conference or sent their representatives. Our plea is that all Panchayati Raj Systems stand to benefit from the experience of others. I have not called this Conference to ask you to rubber stamp our preconceived proposals or to present you with a *fait accompli.* We are interested in your views. We would like to know what you have to say. Let me outline to you our tentative thinking on different aspects of Panchayati Raj. Your comments would be valuable in helping us reach a conclusion.

Our Parliamentary and Assembly elections have invariably been held on time. The Constitution specifies the period within which elections must be held. In stark contrast, elections to Panchayati Raj Institutions have been irregular, frequently postponed and inordinately delayed. There are only a few States where the electoral rhythm for Panchayati Raj Institutions could be said to have matched with that of the Parliamentary and Assembly elections. The States with the longest and most distinguished records are Gujarat and Maharashtra, which have been ruled for most of the last thirty years by Congress Governments. Somewhat less in length of service, but equally distinguished in terms of regularity, has been the case of West Bengal, where regular elections have been a striking feature over more than a decade of CPI (M) rule.

Regular elections of rather more recent vintage have characterised the rule of non-Congress Governments in Andhra Pradesh and Karnataka. The record of some Congress-run Governments, for holding elections, has not been unblemished. Nor is the record of non-Congress Governments, for holding elections, uniform. This is not a matter of political affiliation or political inclination.

The basic reason, for which elections to Parliament and the State Legislatures have been regular, is that they are mandated by the Constitution. The basic reason for irregularity in Panchayat elections has been that these elections are governed by State law and not sanctioned by the Constitution. There would appear to be every need to assure democratic elections in the Panchayats through Constitutional sanction for their periodicity, supervision and control.

The other striking difference between the composition of Parliament and State Legislatures, on the one hand, and Panchayati Raj Institutions, on the other, is that Constitutional provision has been made for the reservation of seats for Scheduled Castes and Scheduled Tribes in the two upper tiers of our democracy but not at the level of Panchayati Raj Institutions. It is this anomaly, more than any other, which is responsible for the gross under-representation in Panchayati Raj Institutions of representatives of these weaker sections. There would appear to be no reason in principle why we should not extend the principle of Constitutional protection for Scheduled Castes and Scheduled Tribes to Panchayati Raj Institutions.

We have also seen that women are under-represented in Panchayati Raj Institutions. This is most unfortunate as it is women who undertake much more than half the economic activities of rural India. It is women to whom is entrusted the welfare and, often, the finances of the household. It is the women of rural India who are the main repository of India's great cultural traditions, of the moral values which are fundamental to the survival and efflorescence of our civilization. Even as we made a beginning for reservations for Scheduled Castes and Scheduled Tribes in the upper tiers, and are now bringing it down to the lower tier, should we not begin the process of reservations for women at the lower tier in the hope that it might in due course expand upwards to the higher tiers?

In most Panchayati Raj Systems, where reservations exist for Scheduled Castes, Scheduled Tribes and women, there is a tendency to fill these posts by nomination, co-option or other forms of indirect representation. The unrepresentative character of many Scheduled Caste, Scheduled Tribe and women representatives in Panchayati Raj Institutions has been emphasised at the various *Sammelans* we have recently held. In Parliament and in our assemblies, the principle has been enshrined that reserved seats, must be filled through direct election from reserved constituencies. It is a principle which must be extended to Panchayati Raj Institutions as a whole. We would wish to introduce a uniform system of reservations for Scheduled Castes, Scheduled Tribes and women in all Panchayati Raj Institutions at all levels throughout the country. Recognizing the great diversity of India, we would like to restrict the principle of uniformity to the inescapable minimum: Beyond the basic principles, which must be uniform throughout the country, we would like to leave it to State Legislatures to determine the electoral law for Panchayati Raj as best suits conditions, locally obtaining in the States. The system of elections for Parliament and for the State Legislatures sanctified by our Constitution is the direct election of members to represent territorial constituencies, by the electorate at large, on the basis of universal adult suffrage. This is a basic principle which we would like to see extended to all the three tiers of the Panchayati Raj System, at the district the intermediate and the village panchayat levels. The Constitution has listed the subjects which fall within the competence of the Centre, those that are entrusted to the States, and those for which the Centre and the States have a joint responsibility. Since Panchayati Raj Institutions do not have legislative responsibilities, there would be no need to add a district list to the existing three lists. But there is need to pool together the experience of devolution in all our different States and prepare an illustrative or minimum list of subjects which, through State legislation, would constitute the basis for a real devolution of power and responsibilities to Panchayati Raj Institutions. Too often in the past, the devolution of administrative powers has been leached of all meaning by the failure to match administrative devolution with financial devolution. It is not enough to endow Panchayats with powers. They also have to be endowed with the means to effectively utilize their powers. At the same time, it will not do to relegate the Panchayats to mere recipients of financial largesse. That would be a recipe for financial indiscipline and irresponsible decision-making. What is equally essential is to inculcate in the Panchayats a deep sense of fiscal responsibility.

As our Constitution stands, legislative authority is given only to Parliament and the State Legislatures. Therefore, the Panchayats cannot acquire fiscal responsibility by the exercise of fiscal legislative powers. They can only acquire fiscal responsibility through being authorised by State Legislatures to levy, collect and appropriate the revenues from specified taxes, duties, fees and tolls. The key word here is: appropriation.

Once a Panchayat knows that it can retain and put to its own use the revenues it raises, there is a built-in incentive to raise taxes and establish a link between moneys raised and moneys spent. The incentive will be further enhanced if it is supplemented by a system of matching grants from the State. West Bengal has done very good work in this area.

In addition to being authorised to appropriate the proceeds of some taxes, it would only be appropriate that the proceeds of some other taxes, duties, tolls and fees be assigned to the Panchayats. This will give them an assured source of revenue and thus, well defined parameters within which to plan projects, programmes and schemes tailored to cut their coats according to the cloth available.

In addition, of course, there have to be grants-in-aid from the Consolidated Funds of the States. The greater the extent of untied funds so granted, the greater would be the authority and autonomy of the Panchayati Raj Institutions to promote forms of development which respond to the articulated needs of the people.

There is no question of either the Constitution or the Centre determining which are the taxes which may be assigned to, or appropriated by the Panchayati Raj Institutions. Nor would it fall within the province of the Constitution or the Centre to determine what proportion of grants-in-aid from the Consolidated Fund of the States should flow to Panchayati Raj Institutions and in what form. However, there have to be objective principles and criteria on the basis of which State Legislatures and State Governments will make such a determination. To facilitate the evolution of such principles, we would like to adopt the innovation begun by the Janata Government in Karnataka of establishing a State Finance Commission.

So far, we have concentrated our attention on democracy and development through institutions of local government in rural India. Clearly, this is only about half our task. We have to bring parallel changes into the administration of metropolitan corporations, municipal committees, town areas, notified areas and other urban and semi-urban conglomerations. The lessons we have learned from the consultations on Panchayati Raj, will be invaluable in helping us determine the Constitutional provisions required to give local government in urban areas of India the same kind of sanctity as we now propose to confer on local government in rural areas of our country.

I would now like to turn to the special problems of certain small and geographically distinctive States and Territories. In at least three States of the North-East, there are extremely vibrant traditional bodies which have been adapted to fulfil the kind of objectives we have in mind for Panchayati Raj Institutions. These are the States of Nagaland, Meghalaya and Mizoram. We would not wish to disturb the traditional system obtaining in these States. Indeed, there is a great deal that Panchayati. Raj Institutions could learn from the democratic and dynamic Village Development Boards of Nagaland.

Then there are areas covered by the Fifth and Sixth Schedules of the Constitution. These too would need special attention to remain insulated, as they have been thus, far from any automatic extension of the Panchayati Raj System. In the same manner, we might have to make special provision for the hill areas of Manipur, which are now governed by the District Council system.

Now that all Union Territories which have the attributes of a State have been given Statehood, the remaining Union Territories—all have distinctive characteristics. In the application of the Panchayati Raj System to these Union Territories, it would be essential to take account of these distinctive characteristics. For example, it would not disturb the system of communes obtaining in Pondicherry or the system of captaincies obtaining in the Nicobar Islands. There will, of course, have to be a well thought out period of transition during which States will be afforded the time and opportunity to modify State Legislation to bring it in conformity with the provisions of the proposed Constitutional amendment. We might also need to enable existing elected Panchayati Raj Institutions to complete their present terms if the State Legislature so decides. These are matters of detail which can be looked into by our draftsmen.

More importantly, the transitional period would have to be availed of by the States to consider the host of supplemental activities required to give full support to the recast, revamped and rejuvenated Panchayati Raj Institutions. The Panchayats would need staff. The officers of the district administration would have to be trained and oriented towards fulfilling their role in the altered political setting. The relationship between the regulatory and development functions of administration will have to be carefully viewed. The blind separation of these functions is a prescription for disaster in a crisis. There has to be some co-ordination and interaction established between the agencies for regulation and the agencies for development, especially in the upper echelons of the district bureaucracy. There also has to be a carefully thought out subordination of officialdom to the elected political authority.

All agencies of planning and development now operating outside the Panchayati Raj System would have to be integrated into the system. Suitable arrangements will have to be thought out for the association with Panchayati Raj Institutions of organisations like co-operatives, marketing organisations and lead banks. One would hope a special effort would be made to bring into the system, voluntary organisations that are involved in the development effort and local resident intellectuals like teachers, lawyers, doctors and others. All these are not matters for Constitutional consideration. They are for State Governments to consider in their discretion. However, we do hope the spirit of the Constitutional amendment will invite consideration by State Governments of these vital and pressing matters of crucial relevance to the successful operation of Panchayati Raj throughout the country.

We are on the threshold of a mighty revolution. It was a revolution envisaged by Jawaharlal Nehru when Panchayati Raj was launched three decades ago. The revolution was not realised because it lacked Constitutional underpinning. We have learnt from experience that Constitutional sanction is as indispensable to democracy at the grassroots as it is to democracy in State Legislatures or in the Parliament of the Union of India. We have also learnt from experience that, even as reservations, as guaranteed by the Constitution, are required to ensure due representation in Parliament and the State Legislatures for the Scheduled Castes and the Scheduled Tribes, so also are such Constitutional guarantees required to ensure due representation in Panchayati Raj Institutions for Scheduled Castes and Scheduled Tribes.

In addition, we have learnt the need to provide access for women to Panchayati Raj Institutions through similar reservations. Finally, we have learnt that Constitutional protection is as essential to devolution to Panchayats as it is to the division of responsibilities between the Union and the States.

This is not a Centre-State issue. We have before us the Sarkaria Commission Report which we are studying to see how to adapt Centre-State relations to evolving circumstances. This is an issue in which the Centre and the States have a common responsibility and a common obligation deriving from Article 40 of the Constitution. It is an obligation deriving also from the ancient "village republics" of our land, so beloved of Gandhiji, deriving also from the emphasis which Panditji gave to planning from the village upwards, deriving too from the revolutionary principles which Indiraji espoused.

Nor is this an issue between the Congress and other political parties. We, in the Congress Party, believe that we have much to learn from our own experience and much also to learn from the experience of Governments run by the Opposition political parties. We acknowledge our debt to the work undertaken by the CPI(M) in West Bengal, the Telugu Desam Party in Andhra Pradesh and the Janata Party in Karnataka. By the same token, we also acknowledge our debt to the work undertaken by Congress Governments in several different parts of the country, including, in particular, our two paragons of Panchayati Raj: Gujarat and Maharashtra.

We have pooled together this experience and churned it. Out of this *manthan* we hope will emerge the nectar to be shared by all the Panchayati Raj Institutions. The basic structure of the Constitution is left unaffected. There is no change proposed in either the State List or the Concurrent List. There is no dilution proposed in the authority of the States. There is no diminution proposed in the legislative competence of State Legislatures. What we do propose is to usher in a revolution by according to Panchayati Raj a status commensurate with the vision of our freedom fighters, the injunctions of our founding fathers and the dreams of our nation-builders.

It is a revolution that will bring democracy to the doorsteps of crores of Indians. It is a revolution that will bring development to lakhs of our villages. It is a revolution that will open the doors of opportunity to millions of Scheduled Castes and Scheduled Tribes, and half the population of our country—the women of India. It is a revolution that will involve the people in their own development. It is a revolution that will replace paternalistic administration with administration by-the people. It is a revolution that will end administration by whimsy. It is a revolution that will make administration representative, responsible and, therefore, responsive.

It is a revolution based on maximum democracy and maximum devolution. It is a revolution to put power in the hands of the people. To this great national task of the highest national importance, I now have the honour to invite each of you to make your contribution.

7

Power to the People

Democracy was the greatest gift of our freedom struggle to the people of India. Independence made the nation free. Democracy made our people free.

A free people are a people who choose their own representatives. A free people are a people who are governed by their will and ruled with their consent. A free people are a people who participate in decisions affecting their lives and their destinies.

Gandhiji believed that democratic freedoms have to be founded in institutions of self-government in every village of India. He drew his inspiration and his vision from the Panchayats, the traditional "village republics" of India. Panditji established the institutions of Panchayati Raj as the primary instrument for bringing development to the doorstep of rural India. Indiraji stressed the need for the people's participation in the processes of economic and social transformation.

Yet, there is no denying that, in most parts of the country, we have failed to fulfil the high hopes we had vested thirty years ago in the institutions of Panchayati Raj. Elections have been irregular. They are often unnecessarily delayed and frequently postponed.

This is not a matter of political will. The best record of regular elections to Panchayati Raj Institutions is of two State Governments which, since the inception of Panchayati Raj, have almost continuously been ruled by the Congress Party: Gujarat and Maharashtra. In recent times, some State Governments run by Opposition parties, such as the CPI (M) in West Bengal, the Telugu Desam Party in Andhra Pradesh and the Janata Party in Karnataka, have held regular elections. In other States, the record of non-Congress parties and coalitions has not been much better than that of Congress-run State Governments. This is not a matter of political parties.

The essence of democracy is elections. Elections to Panchayati Raj Institutions have been woefully irregular and uncertain. A mandatory provision in the Constitution is sacrosanct. A statutory provision in the State law does not quite have the same sanctity. We propose through this will to enshrine in the Constitution regular, periodic elections to Panchayati Raj Institutions. We also propose through this Bill to end the other sickness which has overtaken Panchayati Raj in many parts of the country. That is the sickness of unending suspensions and dissolutions. In the absence of any compelling provision to reconstitute Panchayats within a reasonable period of time, by democratic elections, suspended Panchayats have remained suspended for years on end, and dissolved Panchayats have remained dissolved for a decade and more. In the existing municipal law on the subject, State Legislatures have given the executive authority such wide powers to abort the institutions of Panchayati Raj, and delay reconstituting them, that these institutions have been leached of their ability to stand on their own as representative forums of the people's will. Their existence has depended less on the mandate of the people than the whims of State Governments.

Our Bill leaves it to the States to determine the grounds and conditions on which Panchayats may be suspended or dissolved. We expect State Legislatures to specify the grounds on which the Governor may suspend or dissolve a Panchayat. That is a matter for the Governor acting, in accordance with the Constitution, on the aid and advice of the State Government. Our concern is to ensure that a dissolved Panchayat is reconstituted within a reasonable period of time.

Our Bill would make it mandatory through the Constitution for all Panchayats dissolved before the expiry of their term of office to be reconstituted through democratic elections based on adult suffrage within six months of the dissolution to complete the remaining term. No more will Panchayats remain the plaything of the arbitrary exercise of executive power. It is the people who will determine, within a matter of months, the profile of the reconstituted Panchayat.

It is the Constitution which ensures that the Lok Sabha and the State Assemblies are constituted by the vote of the people on the basis of universal adult suffrage. It is the Constitution which ensures, that, if an Assembly is dissolved. it is reconstituted by a procedure and within a time-frame specified in the Constitution itself. These are essential safeguards to ensure the strength and vitality of democratic institutions. The institutions of Panchayati Raj have lacked strength and vitality precisely because they have lacked Constitutional safeguards.

Our Bill will ensure that Panchayati Raj has a democratic character similar to the Lok Sabha and the State Assemblies and Constitutional protection for their functioning as representative institutions of the people.

The single greatest event in the evolution of democracy in India was the enactment of the Constitution which established democracy in Parliament and in the State Legislatures. This historic, revolutionary Bill takes its place alongside that great event as the enshrinement in the Constitution of democracy at the grassroots.

Till now, there have been weaknesses in the structure of our democracy because, although the superstructure is strong, the foundation has been weak.

Putting together both Houses of Parliament and all the State Legislatures, we have only about 5000 to 6000 persons representing a population of nearly 800 million.

This has had two serious consequences. First, the number of persons holding elective office in well-founded institutions of democracy has been far too small in relation to the size of our electorate. Once we accord to democracy in the Panchayats the same sanctity as is now enjoyed by Parliament and the State Legislatures, we will be opening the doors to the participation in democratic institutions of something like seven lakh elected representatives. The people's stake in democracy will be increased by a factor of approximately one hundred and fifteen.

There is a second deleterious consequence of the vast chasm that separates the general body of the electorate from the small number of its elected representatives. This gap has been occupied by the power-brokers, the middlemen, the vested interests. For the minutest municipal function, the people have had to run around finding persons with the right connections who would intercede for them with the distant sources of power. The system has been captured by the power-brokers. It is being operated in the interests of the power-brokers. It is being protected by the power-brokers. The power-brokers have established their vice-like grip only because democracy has not functioned at the grassroots. The only way of breaking their stranglehold is for democracy to fill the vacuum which the power-brokers have occupied. Once the people have their own elected representatives from electorates as small as a hundred to five hundred persons, the source of power will lie only as far away as the Panchayat Ghar, not some distant State capital or even more distant capital of the country.

To end any role for power-brokers in the system, the Bill provides for the direct election of members to Panchayats at all levels. Every voter will have his own representative in the Gram Panchayat, the mid-level Panchayat, and the Zila Panchayat. That representative will be responsible to a small and well-recognised electorate. If he fulfils the mandate of the people, he will be re-elected. If he fails, the people will throw him out of office. The power of the vote will become the power of enforcement. The will of the people will render the power-broker superfluous.

Today, opportunity for democratically elected leadership is confined to the few thousands who succeed in entering the portals of the State Legislatures and the Parliament. Once this Bill becomes an integral part of the Constitution, a huge, country-wide reservoir of leadership potential will be created. At each Panchayat election, approximately half a crore men and women, most of them young, will present themselves to the electorate seeking the people's mandate. Some will succeed and some will fall by the wayside. Those who do not succeed will get another opportunity five years later.

There is a vast uncultivated field of talent lying fallow in rural India. It is that fallow field we now propose to seed. That field will be watered by the votes of the Members of this House and of your colleagues in Rajya Sabha. The crop of talent you raise will give us the bountiful harvest to take our nation forward to a prosperous, glorious future. There is no country richer than ours in the most precious asset of humankind—the human resource. We, in India, have not flourished as we should because we have not nurtured our greatest resource. This Bill makes it possible for the bulk of the nation's talent to be given opportunity. Throughout the country, there will be a ferment. In everyone of our six hundred thousand villages, in everyone of our five thousand blocks, in everyone of our four hundred districts, democracy will groom the men and women whose experience will subsequently become available to Legislatures at the State level and to the Parliament of the Union of India.

Our proposed Constitutional amendment lays the Constitutional injunction upon the State Legislatures. It is for the State Legislatures to enact the appropriate law. A quite unnecessary controversy has been raised about the role of the Governor in the proposed Panchayati Raj System. The Constitution is unambiguous on this point.

Article 154(1) states that: "The executive power of the State shall be vested in the Governor". Article 163(1) clarifies that: "There shall be a Council of Ministers with the Chief Minister at the head to aid and advise the Governor in the exercise of his functions..." Therefore, the word Governor in the Constitution refers to the Governor exercising his executive powers only and exclusively on the aid and advice of the Council of Ministers, with one exception. The exception is provided for in the remainder of Clause (1) of Article 163, which reads: "...except insofar as (the Governor) is by or under this Constitution required to exercise his functions or any of them in his discretion".

The distinction between the expression "the Governor" and the expression "the Governor in his discretion" is such a well-known matter of Constitutional law that it is amazing there should be any confusion on this point. After all, the expression, "the Governor", appears at scores of places throughout the Constitution and has nowhere been misconstrued or misinterpreted. We are confident that in this Parliament, acting in the exercise of its inherent constituent powers, there will be no confusion between the functions of a Governor acting in accordance with the aid and advice of his Council of Ministers and of a Governor acting in his discretion wherever the Constitution requires him to do so.

In establishing the institutions of democracy in Parliament and in the State Legislatures, our founding fathers gave particular recognition to the disabilities suffered by the Scheduled Castes and the Scheduled Tribes. Provision was made for the reservation of seats for them in accordance with the proportion of their population in the total electorate. This is a principle which has not been incorporated in most of the Panchayati Raj legislations enacted by the State Legislatures.

In my discussions with Panchayati Raj representatives, both during my extensive tours of rural India and in the numerous Panchayati Raj *Sammelans* we have held, it was brought home to me most forcefully that the democratic rights of the Scheduled Castes and the Scheduled Tribes cannot be secured by good intentions alone. At this stage, it has to be secured, in the first instance, by reservations in Panchayati Raj institutions on the same basis as reservations are given in the Lok Sabha and the State Assemblies. I see that a certain section of the House is not happy about this. There is a widespread and justified apprehension on the part of the Scheduled Castes and the Scheduled Tribes that if their due representation in these bodies is not assured, Panchayati Raj could become an instrument of oppression in the hands of the rural elite. Experience in different parts of the country has shown how, in the absence of reservations, vested interests and feudal interests have been able to capture these institutions. Their hold on these institutions has been reinforced by the failure to hold regular elections. The people's mandate has been perverted into an instrument of exploitation.

To forestall such a perversion of the process, our Bill proposes to make it mandatory for State Legislatures to ensure reservation for the Scheduled Castes and the Scheduled Tribes in proportion to their population in the relevant Panchayat area. Our Bill also proposes a significant departure from the Constitution as it exists today. We propose the reservation in Panchayats at all levels of 30 per cent of the seats for women.

There are three major reasons for which we believe this Constitutional innovation to be necessary. First, women constitute half the population and are involved in rather more than half the economic life of rural India. However, to our shame, their share of assets and income is much less than their share of the population but the toil and sweat imposed upon them is rather more than half. Second, the sound finance of the household has traditionally been the responsibility of the women. Financial discipline and fiscal responsibility are ingrained in the habits and outlook of the women of rural India.

These are qualities badly needed in Panchayati Raj Institutions. We believe the presence of women in large numbers in the Panchayats will not only make the Panchayats more representative but will also make them more efficient, honest, disciplined and more responsible. Third, it is the women of India, in their role as grandmothers and mothers, who have been the repository of India's ancient culture and traditions. It is to them that is entrusted the responsibility of transmitting to the next generation the quintessential values, standards and ideals which have enabled our civilization to survive and flourish without a break despite vicissitudes of many kinds. It is that strength of moral character which women will bring to the Panchayats. Let us give them a warm welcome.

I now turn to the heart of the matter: devolution and sound finance. Respecting the right of the States to legislate provisions for devolution, we have deliberately refrained from tampering with their rights. We have no intention of attempting to rule the districts from the Centre. But we do expect the State Legislatures to enact such measures as are required to devolve powers and authority upon the Panchayats, keeping in mind the provisions of this Bill and the spirit in which this Amendment is being brought forward.

First is the power and authority of the Panchayats to draw up plans within the framework of guidelines and conditions to be stipulated by the State Governments. These plans will constitute the basic inputs for the planning process at higher levels. Thus will we ensure that the voice of the people, their felt needs, their aspirations, their priorities become the building blocks of the edifice of planning. We must put an end to planning from above. We must put an end to priorities being conceived and decided at ethereal heights, far removed from the realities on the ground. We must put an end to paternalistic planning. We must initiate a process of people's planning.

Our Bill goes beyond merely planning for economic development. It lays upon the Panchayats even heavier responsibility of planning for social justice. It will not do to romanticise life in our villages. Life there is hard. Life there is exacting. Life there is, in many ways, exploitative and oppressive.

In driving the power-brokers out of the power-houses, in rendering the Panchayats to the people, we lay upon the people's representatives the solemn responsibility of turning their attention, first and foremost, to the needs of the poorest, the most deprived and the most in need. Each plan for economic development will be accompanied by a plan for social justice. No plan for economic development will merit attention until its social justice component is clear. This is a charter not merely for our villages to become prosperous but also for our villages to become just.

The second major responsibility of the Panchayats will be the implementation of development schemes assigned to them by the State Governments on such conditions as may be specified by the State Governments. These schemes should cover the major economic concerns of rural India, commencing with agriculture and land improvement and going on to irrigation and watershed management. It must comprise the diversification of the rural economy into animal husbandry, dairying, poultry and fisheries. It must incorporate industrial activity in rural India. It must extend to minor forest produce, which is the chief source of income for our entire tribal populace. It must encompass the day-to-day concerns of rural India: housing, drinking water, fuel and fodder. Devolution must deal with the basic infrastructure of communication and power in rural India. We have suggested the inclusion in the Panchayats' area of competence, development schemes relating to non-conventional energy sources.

The proposed Eleventh Schedule seeks to vest in the Panchayats, the major responsibility for the administration of poverty-alleviation programmes. It would entrust the Panchayats with education and culture, as well as health and family welfare, woman and child development. We propose to request the State Legislatures to make social welfare programmes for all the weaker and handicapped sections, a functional responsibility of the Panchayats. We also propose to give to the Panchayats the responsibility for the public distribution system, which is so crucial to the survival of the weakest and the poorest, as also to the general health of the rural economy.

The Bill proposes that the Panchayats be entrusted with the most neglected area of our community life, namely the maintenance of community assets. I would like to stress that the Eleventh Schedule is not an exhaustive list. We hope that the States will progressively devolve many more powers and authority upon the Panchayats so that whatever can be looked after at the local level is looked after at that level and not remitted upstairs.

The single greatest danger we have to guard against is the devolution of powers to the Panchayats being followed by the transfer of these powers out of the Panchayati Raj System into other bodies constituted outside the system and placed under the direct control of State Governments. Almost all State Governments, whether Congress or non-Congress, who have established a good system of Panchayati Raj have seriously weakened the impact by constituting bodies outside the Panchayati Raj System where real powers of decision-making are vested and where the elected representatives of Panchayati

Raj are overshadowed by Ministers appointed by the State Governments or, as in the case of Karnataka, by the MLA becoming the *ex-officio* Chairman of the Taluka Panchayat Samiti.

It is the purpose of our Bill to ensure that powers delegated to the Panchayats remain within the Panchayats and are not channelled outside the system. By the same token, our Bill is designed to ensure that all development agencies are brought within the framework of the Panchayati Raj Institutions and made responsive to the elected authority. There are two basic reasons for administration at the district and sub-district levels having become so unresponsive to the people. One is the fragmentation of the district administration into a large number of agencies vertically owing responsibility to State Governments without adequate co-ordination at a single focal point at the district level. The other has been the absence of an elected authority to function at that focal point.

The House would recall that our Government was returned to office with the largest mandate ever accorded to any party in the history of Independent India. I, as Head of that Government, pledged to make a number of structural changes. I very quickly discovered that the system could not cope with the demands which we were making upon it. There was too much ossification. Mere tinkering with the system would not do a systemic transformation was essential. Indeed, the starting point of the exercise which has led to the presentation of this Bill was my search for a way of fulfilling the 20th point of our revised 20-Point Programme of 1986, which promised to the people a responsive administration. At my instance, the Department of Personnel organised a series of Workshops on Responsive Administration to which were invited all the District Magistrates, Deputy Commissioners and Collectors of the country. I spent over 20 hours in discussion with them.

It emerged that we could not make our administration responsive merely by simplifying procedures or establishing grievance redressal machinery or opening complaint windows. Every such step only led to the one more power centre for the power-brokers to occupy. The *sine qua non* of responsive administration is representative administration, responsible to the electorate. Such responsive administration in rural India can only be secured through genuine Panchayati Raj. It is this that our Bill seeks to achieve. Devolution of administrative powers must go hand-in-hand with sound finance. Too often in the past, Panchayati Raj has had functions without finances, responsibilities without funds, duties without the means of carrying them out. Our Bill empowers State Legislatures to ensure the sound finance of the Panchayats by endowing them with the revenues of taxes that might be appropriated by, or assigned to them, as also with grants-in-aid from the Consolidated Fund of the State. To assist State Legislatures and the executive authority in determining which taxes to assign or leave for appropriation, as also the grants-in-aid to be given, the Bill proposes the establishment of a Finance Commission to make suitable recommendations.

I would stress the importance of determining the taxes which will be levied, collected and appropriated by the Panchayats. Nothing will inculcate in the Panchayats a greater sense of fiscal responsibility than the possibility of retaining with them the moneys that they raise for such use as they best deem fit. United grants make for local-level planning. Authorisation for appropriation makes for responsible local-level planning. So far, the tendency has been to confine appropriation to cesses. We hope State Legislatures will go further and identify taxes, duties, tolls and fees which might be appropriated by the Panchayats.

We are asking the State Legislatures no more than we are ourselves ready to do as a Union Government. A beginning has been made with the Jawahar Rozgar Yojana. Eighty per cent of the funds are being devolved on the village Panchayats. We propose to extend this principle to other Centrally-sponsored schemes. There can be no better way of involving the people in their own development. There can be no better way of reducing corruption and nepotism. The system we propose is a transparent system. The bulk of the electorate in a village is composed of the intended beneficiary of development schemes. Each intended beneficiary will know what schemes are available, how much money there is in the scheme, whether and how the moneys are being spent. Any *Panch* or *Sarpanch* who cheats the people will be removed by the people. There is no way he can escape the consequences of malfeasance.

I would now like to turn to those parts of the country we are proposing to exempt from the system, or in respect of which special provision is made for modification. In the North-East, there is one sparsely populated tribal State which has no difficulty in adopting Panchayati Raj without modification. This is the State of Arunachal Pradesh. The Bill recognises that in three other States of the North-East—Nagaland, Meghalaya and Mizoram—there are traditional systems of self-government, akin to Panchayati Raj, which must be preserved. Indeed, the rest of the country would be well-advised to study and learn from the Village Development Boards of Nagaland. In these three States, the traditional systems will be left undisturbed.

Similarly, in areas covered by the Sixth Schedule, where autonomous District Councils have been established, we would not wish to disturb the system so carefully structured. On the same principle, we are not extending the Bill to the District Council areas of Manipur and the areas covered by the Gorkha Hill Council in the Darjeeling district of West Bengal. As regards the Union Territories, the Bill empowers the President to withhold, extend or modify the application of the provisions of the Bill to a part or the whole of the Union Territories. This is designed to ensure that traditional or nascent institutions in areas like the Nicobar Islands, Lakshadweep and Pondicherry are not adversely affected and that the special characteristics of Union Territories like Delhi are taken into account.

Similarly, in tribal areas covered by the Fifth Schedule, the Governor in his discretion (and *not* on advice of his Council of Ministers) may determine the conditions on which Panchayati Raj would be extended to these areas. Sir, the Bill proposes that all State Legislatures bring their State legislation into conformity with the proposed Part IX of the Constitution within a year of the commencement of operation of the amendment. We recognize, however, that Panchayati Raj institutions have been elected in most States, some as recently as this year. The Bill authorizes the continuance of these Panchayats till the expiry of their terms, unless State Legislatures decide otherwise.

The interregnum between the passage of this Bill and the alignment of State legislation with its provisions will, we hope, be used by State Governments to give deep thought to the working of the new system. Panchayats will have to be given the staff they require. We do not propose that the annual confidential reports of the bureaucracy be written by elected representatives at the Panchayat level but the district bureaucracy will have to be trained and oriented towards discharging its new responsibilities in changed conditions. We have to build trust and mutual respect between the district bureaucracy and the elected Panchayats. At other levels of our democracy, in the States and at the Centre, the bureaucracy and the elected authority have learnt to work together in mutual co-operation. Such a harmonious relationship must also subsist between the district bureaucracy and the Panchayats. We hope State Governments will resist the temptation to effect a cleavage between the regulatory and development functions of district administration. There will have to be co-ordination because it is only through development administration that a regulating officer can establish the contacts and linkages essential to forestalling a law-and-order crisis or resolving it when it occurs.

We are deeply conscious, Sir, that this Bill restricts itself to democracy and development at the grassroots in rural India. We must extend the same concern to the growing urban and semi-urban population of the country. To this end, Government proposes to bring forward major legislation in the next session of the Lok Sabha. We shall also turn our attention to recasting, revamping and rejuvenating the co-operative movement, which Panditji had always regarded as the essential complement to Panchayati Raj.

Mr. Speaker, Sir, we come to this House after long consideration and a national debate without precedent. We have consulted with more than ten thousand representatives of Panchayati Raj Institutions from all over the country. We have discussed Panchayati Raj with the bureaucracy at different echelons, including district officers, Chief Secretaries and

Secretaries to the Government of India. We have held meetings with Panchayati Raj Ministers and the Chief Ministers of the States. We have extended the debate to political levels, within Party forums and in a Parliamentary Consultative Committee. Our proposals are before you but our mind is not closed. In the months to come, we hope there will be intensive debate about these proposals all over the country. We are prepared to carry forward such discussions with Opposition parties and Chief Ministers. We will, of course, listen with the utmost care to suggestions made on the floor of the House. We seek consensus, but we are prepared to face the challenge of confrontation. We shall fight for democracy for the people. We shall fight for development for the people. It is the people of India who are our first and foremost concern.

The proposals we place before the House are not really our proposals. They are the proposals of the people of India. We have drawn on the accumulated experience of Panchayati Raj from all over the country, the good experience as well as the bad, the experience of Congress-run Governments as much as of State Governments run by other parties. This experience has been pooled and churned. Out of this *manthan* has emerged the *amrit* which we now propose to share.

Our democracy has reached the stage where the full participation of the people brooks no further delay. We are accused of rushing through this Bill. There has been no rush. For several years now, we have been holding well-publicised consultations at several different levels on Panchayati Raj. No one in the public life of this country could have been unaware of our intentions. Our respected Rashtrapatiji, in his address to both Houses of Parliament, had specifically referred to the major legislation on the subject which Government proposed to bring forward. We now fulfil that promise. Those who decry this as an election gimmick are precisely those whose feudal interests will be overthrown by power reaching the people. We trust the people. We have faith in the people. It is the people who must determine their own destinies and the destiny of the nation. To the people of India, let us ensure maximum democracy and maximum devolution. Let there be an end to the power-brokers. Let us give power to the people.

8

Towards a Responsive and Representative Municipal Administration

The leadership of our freedom movement was in many ways nurtured in the civic bodies. Among the stalwarts who, so to speak, cut their teeth on municipal administration were Dadabhai Naoroji and Pherozeshah Mehta, Tilak and Gokhale, Chittaranjan Das and Subhas Bose, and Panditji.

Panditji was particularly enthused with the kind of grassroots work involved in democratic municipal administration. He said in words that are perhaps even more relevant today than when he spoke: "Corporations and municipalities seem to bring one in more intimate touch with the life of the people... When you go to Delhi, you get farther away from the common man, sitting, as it were, on some legislative mountain top... The poor people are sometimes completely forgotten... Government departments grow, till one department hardly knows and recognizes the other or becomes jealous of the other."

The commencement of our freedom struggle virtually coincided in time with Lord Ripon's attempt in 1882 to organise local self-government in urban India. Interestingly, from 1882 till Independence the proportion of our urban population to the total population remained virtually the same, at something under 10 per cent. Through much of this period, the total urban population of India was not much more than that of Greater

Bombay alone today. India, as Gandhiji said, lived in her villages and it is to democratic local self-government in rural India that Gandhiji concentrated his attention. Therefore, although the municipalities were the nurseries of administrative experience for our freedom fighters, the role of municipalities in the life of the nation was limited.

However, in the four decades that we have been free and independent, the demographic profile of the country has changed vastly. Already, almost a quarter of our population is urbanised and the number of Indians living in urban settlements is nearly 200 million. The urban population is growing at around 4 per cent per annum, as against 1.5 per cent for the rural population. By the turn of the century, something like one Indian in three will be living in urban India. Inevitably, this proportion will grow till, as in developed countries, around 3/4 of the population will become urban, leaving not much more than a quarter in the rural countryside. It, therefore, becomes incumbent on us to confer on urban India the same kind of advantages and benefits of democracy and devolution as we are seeking to secure for rural India through the Panchayati Raj Bill.

It is our expectation that the development process will receive a new impetus and a new thrust through democratic decentralization. Planning will become more finely-tuned to the needs of the people and the realities on the ground. Implementation will become more efficient and less prone to corruption through the involvement of the people and their representatives at the grassroots level. Since urbanization constitutes one of the most important motors of growth and modernization, it follows that the development benefits of democratic decentralization require the process to incorporate urban as much as rural areas. Also, it is growth in the towns and cities that comprises many of the agents of change and transformation. For change to be democratic and transformation to be cognizant of ground realities, Panchayati Raj is as much an urban need as a rural requirement.

We have before us three options for urban renewal. One is to leave the system and structure as it is and pray that it will somehow dynamize itself, by a process of internal combustion, as it were. To do so would, however, be utterly unrealistic. Urban local bodies are in as advanced a stage of decay as the management of urban development is in crying need of rejuvenation. In these circumstances, persistence with the *status quo* would be nothing short of a prescription for disaster.

The second option would be for the Centre to resume all powers for urban development and push through its plans for change by direction and enforcement from above. I have no doubt that this could be done efficiently but it would not be democratic. I would prefer to trust the people and their elected representatives.

This brings us to the only remaining option, the third option which we are now pursuing, that is, Constitutional sanction for ensuring democracy in urban local bodies and Constitutional sanction to endow them with the responsibilities and finances required to ensure that urban India flourishes and leads the country forward to progress and prosperity.

How far removed urban local self-government is from present realities might be gauged from the fact that the essential structure of such self-government is seven years older than Jawaharlal Nehru, whose centenary we are celebrating this year. A structure conceived in imperial times for a relatively tiny urban population, which was almost wholly dependent on the requirements of imperial administration and imperial trade, has persisted through four decades of freedom. In the Constitution, while the Directive Principles of State Policy refer, albeit glancingly, to village Panchayats, the reference to urban local self-government is confined to an implicit mention in Entry Five of the State List.

The consequences of the absence of adequate Constitutional provision for urban local self-government can be seen in the mess in which municipal administration in much of the country finds itself. More than half the Corporations stand suspended. Some of the suspensions, as in the case of Madras and Lucknow, stretch back to 15 or 16 years. The Bhagalpur Corporation heads the list, having been suspended eighteen years ago. That is, the youngest vote who will cast his vote in the next general election was born after the Bhagalpur Corporation was superseded!

This is not a matter of political party or political persuasion. If it is a fact that three-quarters of the suspended Corporations are in States run by the Congress Party, it is equally a fact that three-quarters of the Corporations that are in operation are also operating in Congress-run States. Prolonged and arbitrary suspension is not the consequence of party policy. It is the consequence of a weak Constitutional base for local self-government.

The Panchayati Raj Bill, which I introduced in Parliament on the 15th May 1989, holds out the promise of maximum democracy and maximum devolution to 75 per cent of our population which lives in rural India.

There is no reason in principle, and every reason in equity, for these essential democratic rights to also reach our rapidly growing urban population. The concept of Panchayati Raj must change to incorporate the country's changing demographic profile, and must expand to incorporate the country's growing urban population.

That is not merely a matter of figures and ratios. Impulses for the generation of wealth, income and employment are strongest in urban centres. Much of the country's best talent is being attracted to our towns and cities. The best educated, the young men and women with entrepreneurial abilities, those willing to take risks, those willing to place the highest stakes upon their own abilities, those with enthusiasm, enterprise, zeal and ambition are migrating in droves from rural to urban India. While we must do something to moderate this inflow and ensure that rural India too enjoys the benefits of this precious human capital, we must at the same time give to these dynamic forces in urban India the democratic voice and participation in development which we have sought to ensure for rural India through the Panchayati Raj Bill.

It is to consider how best this might be done that we have called you to this conference. We are beginning the process of consultations with the municipal bureaucracy for the same reason that we began the process of consultations on Panchayati

Raj with the district bureaucracy. Subsequent phases of the consultative process will include the elected representatives of the municipal bodies and the State Governments. The reason we begin with you is that we have reason to believe that you share with the district bureaucracy two characteristics which powerfully impressed me when I participated in the District Magistrates' Workshops on Responsive Administration.

The first was the deep sense of dedication to duty which the district bureaucracy displayed. We know that a similar sense of discipline and devotion characterises the approach of the municipal bureaucracy. Yet, even as the district bureaucracy itself felt that the individual merits of the officers notwithstanding, district administration is insufficiently responsive, sub-optimally efficient, and skewed away from the people's priorities, so also do we imagine the municipal bureaucracy is less than satisfied with the functioning of municipal administration and would wish to suggest ways of making it more responsive, more efficient, and more relevant to the people's needs.

The second characteristic which we noted in the approach of the district bureaucracy was the pervading conviction that responsive district administration is not possible without representative district administration. Twenty or thirty years ago, and certainly before Independence, the Civil Services used to regard the political authority as an interfering nuisance. In contrast, the young men and women of the IAS and the Provincial Civil Services whom we met at the Workshops were almost unanimous in the view that bureaucratic administration, however well-intentioned, is no substitute for democratic administration. It is with their wholehearted backing that we have introduced the Panchayati Raj Bill.

We have reason to believe that the municipal bureaucracy like its counterparts in the district administration, also believes that the *sine qua non* of responsive municipal administration is democratic municipal administration. In the extensive State legislation on the subject, democracy is certainly the intended basis for municipal administration. But, in practice, democracy in municipal administration is either totally abrogated by arbitrary and prolonged suspensions, of is weakened, even nullified, by various provisions which dilute the representative character of these bodies. There is the device of nomination and other such non-representational means of packing these bodies. There is the vesting of effective powers of decision-making in non-elected officials. There is the host of agencies that have sprung up outside the framework of democratically-elected municipal bodies to undertake not only the discretionary tasks of these bodies but even many of their obligatory tasks.

We would like you to advise us on how best we can make maximum democracy and maximum devolution, the *leitmotif* of our municipal administration.

At this stage of the consultative process, we have no proposals to put to you. We only have issues which we would like to pose for your consideration. We are open to suggestions regarding other issues which you think might be germane to our tasks. There is a substantial body of literature on the subject. There are the background papers to this conference which are in your hands. But above all, we look to your rich personal experience to gain an understanding and an insight into the steps that must be taken to make municipal administration responsive, representative and responsible.

The first set of issues relates to the structure of municipal administration. The practice varies widely from one part of the country to the other. There is generally no accepted set of criteria regarding even what constitutes an urban agglomeration, let alone the manner in which it should be run.

At what stage, in your opinion, does a rural area start assuming an urban character? Is this merely a question of population—or are there other factors which would warrant a rural area being redesignated as urban? Further, are the existing gradations from a notified area to town to municipality to corporation appropriate and adequte? Indeed, are they meaningful at all? If they are, should there be some uniformity in determining the criteria which would distinguish, say, a town area committee from municipality?

Associated with this is the question of uniformity and diversity. Given a country as geographically diverse as ours is, with wide variations in such key variables as climate, natural geographic features, occupation patterns, density of population, and other factors perhaps it would be best to restrict the search for uniformity to basic principles and leave the rest to the immense variety of the country. But, put this way, the query really begs the question, because the moot point is: what are the basic principles that ought to be uniform?

In the Panchayati Raj System that we envisage for rural India, the basic unit of local self-government is the village Panchayat, with each panch representing an electorate of somewhere between a hundred and five hundred voters.

Such a small electorate ensures ready access for every voter to the elected representative. It also ensures that the basic unit of decision-making and implementation is intimately responsible to the people. There would be a transparency about the administrative actions of the unit because the general body of the electorates is aware of what are the functions that are to be performed. What is the money available for performing these functions, who are the entitled beneficiaries, and whether undue favouritism is being shown or unjustified discrimination is being practised. The system is bound to lead to more efficient implementation, less exploitation, reduced corruption and, we hope, the elimination of nepotism.

By the same token, should not the basic unit of urban administration be the equivalent of a village Panchayat, say, a *mohalla* Panchayat? There are, of course, many dissimilarities between the rural and the urban situation, notably the relative isolation of one village from another compared to the very strong linkages between one *mohalla* and the other, and the integrated nature of most of the services required by an urban agglomeration. Therefore, there can be no mere imitative replication of the village Panchayat in the urban setting. But we would like you to consider what might be the optimal size of population for the basic unit of urban administration, and what might be the functions vested in this unit.

From this follows the question of the remaining levels of urban administration. Would the intermediate Panchayat of the Panchayati Raj Bill find equivalence in the median size of population served by, say, a notified area committee or a town committee? If so, should there be a two-tier system of local self-government for these bodies and, possibly, a three-tier system for Municipalities and Corporations? In considering the questions of levels of local self-government, we would like you to draw on your own experience, the historical experience of urban local self-government in India and other countries, as well as the imperative necessity of ensuring responsive democratic institutions at the grassroots level in urban India as in rural India.

The kind of supersessions we have experienced in municipal administration are incompatible with the norms of democracy. The Panchayati Raj Bill provides for regular elections every five years. It requires dissolved Panchayats to be reconstituted within six months of dissolution to serve out the remainder of the term. And it establishes a system whereby all Panchayats at all levels will simultaneously go to the polls at the expiry of their tenure. Should similar provisions be built into the Bill we are proposing to introduce to set the Constitutional framework for urban local self-government?

Existing practice in regard to reservations for Scheduled Castes and Scheduled Tribes and women in urban local bodies varies considerably from State to State. Some States like Goa, Karnataka, Maharashtra and Rajasthan provide for the reservation of seats for the Scheduled Castes and Scheduled Tribes in proportion to their proportion of the total population. Other States use other formulae. Yet other States have no provisions at all for SC/ST reservations.

As regards reservations for women, no State can claim to have done justice to half of our population. At best, a token number of seats are reserved for women.

There are wide variations in the manner of choosing representatives to fill reserved seats. In some places, this is by straightforward direct election; in many others, by nomination. Much the same position obtains in respect of Corporations, for which most States have separate Acts.

It is impossible for the weaker sections of society to secure adequate representation, full participation and an equitable share of the benefits of municipal administration unless there are reserved seats for SC/STs, at least in proportion to their proportion of the population, and a substantial share of reserved seats for women. Moreover, it is crucial that reserved seats for SC/STs be filled by direct election from reserved constituencies and not by nomination. Similarly, reserved seats for women also need to be filled by direct election and not nomination. How, in your view, should reservations operate?

We would like your views on whether the Chief Executive and his colleagues should be directly elected by the electorate or elected by, and from amongst, the elected members of the local bodies? Also, what in your view should be other forms of representation to be permitted in urban local bodies? Related to this is the issue of whether the Municipal Commissioner or other Municipal officer should be responsible to the elected Chief Executive or to the State Government.

If democracy is to be assured through suitable Constitutional provisions relating to the structure of local administration, elections and reservations, the kernel of responsive administration lies in the powers devolved to municipal bodies.

In the Panchayati Raj Bill, there are two broad stipulations in respect of the devolution of powers. First, plans drawn up by the Panchayats are to constitute the basic inputs for the planning process. Moreover, each Panchayat is to dovetail its plan for economic development into plans for social justice. We would like your views on these two separate but related points in respect of planning at different levels of municipal administration.

We would like you to share with us the role which you envisage for elected local bodies in the planning process. At present, there exist many different agencies outside the framework of democratically elected local bodies, to whom is entrusted most of the major tasks of urban planning. These include City Development Authorities and City Improvement Trusts, besides a number of State agencies, owing responsibilities to the State Government above, but not to the people below. If planning for economic development and social justice is to become the centre piece of the activities of democratic local bodies, should all these other agencies be dissolved or merged into the elected local bodies? Or should they be kept separate and above the system, as at present? The answer you give should be compatible with our basic principle of maximum democracy and maximum devolution.

The second point relating to planning is the methodology for co-ordinating urban planning with rural planning. While it would, of course, be appropriate for urban and rural bodies respectively to plan matters which fall exclusively within their respective jurisdictions, it has to be recognised that growth impulses largely stem from the interaction between urban agglomerations and their rural hinterland. It is because the linkages between town and country are so crucial to growth that many State Governments have established bodies like the District Planning Board or the District Planning and Development Council to identify and strengthen these linkages. The tragedy is that, in the name of co-ordination, District Planning Boards and DPDCs have been established outside the framework of democratically elected local bodies and generally placed under the control of a Minister appointed by the State Government.

Thus, the most crucial planning functions and much of the effective decision-making power, as also the allocation of the bulk of finances, has been vested in bodies which are outside the democratic framework of local government and are dominated by Ministers appointed by the State Government. I call it a tragedy because it is through these agencies that the elected authority is bypassed or over-ruled. In the name of co-ordination, democracy is being sabotaged. In the name of co-ordination the will of elected local bodies is being subordinated to the will of the State Government. In the name of co-ordination, the people's will is being replaced by the will of officialdom.

What measure would you suggest to establish a democratic district planning body that would take account of linkages between town and country in the formulation of district plans? Should such a body be directly elected by the people? Or should the DPDC be elected by an electoral college comprising all the elected members of both the rural and the urban Panchayats? Or should it be composed *ex-officio*? We would need to be guided by your experience in this matter.

The second major act of devolution envisaged in the Panchayati Raj Bill is the implementation of development schemes relating to the subjects set out in the proposed Eleventh Schedule. We would wish you to pool your experience of the different States of India and suggest the subjects which might be set out in a separate Schedule in respect of which Constitutional authority would be available for the meaningful devolution of powers to urban Panchayats.

The financial condition of municipal bodies at all levels is pitiable. They most barely have the funds to sustain themselves. They are unable to even maintain community assets and services, let alone create new ones. Debt and default are widespread. There is fiscal irresponsibility allied to financial indiscipline.

The sound finances of urban institutions of local self-government is a matter of critical importance. Much of the wealth of India is generated in urban India. Its rate of growth are significantly higher than in rural India. The asset which municipal bodies sit on, namely, urban land, is a very valuable commodity whose value goes on increasing rapidly. We would like you to examine in depth all questions relating to the financial health of urban bodies. You have numerous reports on the subject prepared by Committees established by both the Central and State Governments. You have in the Panchayati Raj Bill the proposal for the establishment of a State Finance Commission to set out principles on the basis of which taxes may be assigned to, or appropriated by the Panchayati Raj Institutions at different levels. Then there are the grants-in-aid from the Consolidated Fund of the State and funds from Centrally-sponsored schemes. Should the proposed State Finance Commission also set out similar principles for financial devolution to urban local bodies? Should there be Centrally-sponsored schemes for urban areas? There is also the question of access for municipal bodies to institutional finance and the capital market.

We would like your consideration of these financial questions to be guided by the sentiments expressed by Jawaharlal Nehru when he presented his first report as Chairman of the Allahabad Municipality sixty six years ago. He said: "The first necessity of a municipal administration is financial equilibrium... But we want to stand on our own legs and do not believe in a municipality being habitually carried on promise of doles."

Finally, we would like you to consider issues that are vital for efficient municipal administration but are not, perhaps, amenable to settlement through a Constitutional provision.

For example, what should be the relationship between the municipal bureaucracy and the elected municipal representatives? How does one ensure harmony and co-operative relations between the municipal bureaucracy and the democratically elected representatives of municipal bodies? Should not urban administration be carried out at the behest of the elected representatives rather than by bureaucratic fiat, however benevolent and well-intentioned? And what mechanisms of co-ordination are required between the district bureaucracy and the municipal bureaucracy?

We would also wish you to consider the sort of training and orientation the municipal bureaucracy would require to fit itself in with the new democratic system. In this context, would it be advisable to have a municipal civil service separate from the existing Provincial Civil Service and the IAS?

I am posing several questions. I do not wish to preempt the answers. We have hypothesis in our mind, some of which are implicit in the issues I have raised and in the points set out in the issues paper. But our mind is open. We have not closed any options.

I look forward to spending several hours with you in panel discussions. I hope you will be frank and uninhibited. We seek your advice because we value your advice. We hope you will give us your advice freely and frankly. We shall then carry the debate forward to political levels. The final decisions will, of course, be ours, but they will be based on a consultative process without precedent in regard to either its intensity or its extent.

We are determined to give power to the people. But in determining the mode and modalities of doing so, we wish to begin with the Municipal officers who, by virtue of their experience and expertise, are best suited to set the ball rolling.

9

Demands of a Vibrant Democracy

I welcome to this Conference all Chief Ministers and other representatives of State Governments who have kindly accepted my invitation to attend. I regret the absence of those who have chosen to stay away. Dialogue is the essence of democracy. In giving power to the people, we have engaged in the most extensive process of consultations ever undertaken since Independence. As a Government, we have consulted something like twenty five thousand knowledgeable individuals with personal experience of Panchayati Raj Institutions and urban local bodies. Through Congress Party forums we have reached out to tens of thousands of others. The Conference of Chief Ministers held on the 5th May represented the culmination of the process in regard to Panchayati Raj. This Conference represents the culmination of the consultations in regard to urban local bodies. We regret that some of those who saw reason to participate in the last conference have declined to participate ill this complementary exercise. We particularly regret the absence of those who initially pledged their participation but later allowed their own better judgement to be subordinated to the whimsies of others. We will miss the contribution of all those who are not here, even as we are bound to benefit from the valuable contribution which will be made by those of you whom we now welcome to Delhi.

The tradition of Panchayats as institutions of local self-government is integral to the Indian tradition. It evolved in rural India where, till very recently, almost whole of India lived.

It was a concept that could and should have been adapted to the needs of urban local self-government as urbanization in the country gathered pace. Urbanization, however, coincided with the rise of the British colonial administration. So, models evolved elsewhere were trans posed to this country. They were models designed for Imperial preferences and Imperial prejudices, Imperial cares and Imperial compulsions, the colonial bureaucracy, the colonial military, the colonial merchant and their feudal satraps. We are now engaged in enshrining in the Constitution Mahatma Gandhi's vision of democracy in the village as the foundation on which to erect the superstructures of democracy. It is important that urban India be comprehended within the same effort. There are several reasons for this.

First, we have broken out of the stagnation of colonialism. We have burst through the 3.5 per cent annual growth limit which, at one time, seemed to be an impregnable barrier. We have pushed the economy on to a long-term growth path of 5 per cent and above, a rate of growth which our people have not seen in many centuries. Yet, we need even higher rates of growth, much higher rates of growth. It is not merely a matter of emulating the example of other newly industrialising developing countries who have grown faster than us. It is primarily a matter of meeting our people's aspirations. Performance engenders expectations. Expectations are a function of experience. Precisely because we have done well, our people expect us to do even better. But higher rates of economic transformation cannot be sustained without required adjustments to the political structure. Stability demands sound and well entrenched institutions of democracy. Democracy in Parliament and in the State Legislatures imparted stability to the country's polity as the economy transited from stagnation to modest growth. Now, as the economy moves into higher gear, shifting from modest to ever-higher rates of growth; political stability rests on further entrenching democracy at the foundation, at the level at which the bulk of our people encounter the government. Without such strengthening, the energy released by the propulsion of growth could endanger the superstructure of democracy, which is fragile because our polity is not yet founded in democracy at the grassroots, in democracy where the people live.

Also, democracy cannot long survive paternalistic models of economic growth. A vibrant democracy demands participatory growth. We are making decisions regarding what is good for the people at levels far removed from the people. We are then implementing these plans through a machinery that is alien to the people's will. This has led to a peculiar psychological and sociological syndrome in which the people believe that they have a right to development but not a responsibility for development. The assertion of a right without a recognition of the corresponding responsibility translates into unreal expectations, unrelated to real constraints of resources, unrelated to the inescapable need to make choices between alternative uses, unrelated to the imperative of raising resources, deploying them intelligently among competing needs, and phasing the fulfilment of expectations according to sensibly perceived priorities.

It is by no means the people's fault that this sense of responsibility for their own well-being, progress and growth has not percolated to the grassroots. The fault lies with us in that neither democracy nor the devolution of power nor the assignment of responsibilities has been assured or effectively undertaken at the cutting-edge where the people and the administration meet. This we propose to rectify. For rural India, we have presented to Parliament the Constitution (64th) Amendment Bill. For urban India, we seek your advice on how to bring: maximum democracy and maximum devolution to the doorstep of the urban local bodies.

There are two further reasons of special importance for bringing democracy and devolution to urban India, one statistical, the other of pervasive economic, social and political significance. The statistical point is that in all these five thousand years of civilization, urban settlements have never accounted for much more than a twentieth fraction of our population. However, in the last four decades we have seen the urban population surge to a quarter of our population, that is, something of the order of 200 million people. This trend is irreversible and bound to accelerate. Within the next ten years, one in every three Indians will inhabit urban settlements. Today's youth is likely to see a predominantly urbanised India by the time he/she reaches middle age. Therefore, Panchayati Raj, that is democratic local self-government as envisaged by our sages and seers and as engrained in the traditions of our country and the thought processes of our citizens, must reach not only the hundreds of millions who live in rural India but also the hundreds of millions who are now swelling our towns and cities.

Much more significantly, the compartmentalization of India into sharply delineated rural components and urban enclaves has long ceased to be of real significance. When, over a century ago, Lord Ripon established the basic framework for urban local self-government, town and country inhabited two quite separate worlds. The dynamics of development has changed all that. All over India, there are rural settlements transforming themselves into urban agglomerations. This transformation is often engendered by higher agricultural productivity. Agricultural inputs like fertilizers and pesticides need to be stored and retained. Agricultural implements need to be manufactured and supplied. Agricultural machinery needs to be serviced. Agricultural surpluses need to be marketed. Agricultural produce needs to be processed. When agriculture was almost entirely subsistence farming, a cleavage between town and country was possible. With the monetizing of the agricultural economy, the rural hinterland needs an urban growth point, even as urban prosperity depends on rural growth. There has arisen between the indubitably rural settlements, on the one hand, and the equally indubitable urban agglomeration, on the other a series of transitional settlements which, both in space and time, draw much of their sustenance and logic from the land-based economic activity of the countryside. Reciprocally, without them rural progress would be stalled. We must, therefore, replace the compartmentalization of rural and urban administration, rural and urban development by a rural-urban continuum. A holistic perception is needed to see the thread that links the remotest hamlet to the largest megapolis.

It is only the recognition of this continuum which will enable us to rationally plan the prosperity of whole India. At present, nearly half of India's urban population is concentrated in a few metropolitan centres. Rational urbanisation would mean replacing half-a-dozen major urban magnets by, say, two hundred mini-magnets. We need the smaller urban agglomerations for obvious economic reasons. We also need them for environmental reasons. The rural environment can only be protected by drawing away people whom the land cannot support. But the process of drawing them away would be better to a large number of attractive, well-designed, well-supplied smaller urban agglomerations than the uncontrolled flood now flowing into our cities, wrecking the urban environment. It means each State working on an Urbanisation Plan. It means each State drawing up an Environmental Plan. It means each State preparing an Industrialization Plan. It means the conscious promotion of town planning expertise, with special emphasis on aesthetic values in urban construction. It means making this expertise available to differentiated levels of local self-government all along the rural-urban continuum.

Therefore, instead of just devising a set of structures of local self-government for rural India and a separate set of structures of local self-government for urban India, we require a linking structure, a transitional structure for settlements which are growing out of villages but have not yet quite become full-fledged towns. These transitional structures exist in our municipal laws as notified area committees and town committees. In Gujarat and Tamil Nadu, the transitional structure is the Nagar Panchayat and constitutes a part of the Panchayati Raj Institutions. I shall refer to the transitional structures by the term Nagar Panchayats.

Nagar Panchayats are not merely a matter of administrative convenience or administrative efficiency. It is the inter-relationship between the rural hinterland and the urban growth centre which is the catalyst of growth. The first manifestation of an urban growth centre is the village Panchayat evolving into a Nagar Panchayat. Planning for the rural areas of a district without taking into account the linkages: between these rural areas, and the Nagar Panchayats or urban municipalities constitutes a disservice to both. Optimising economic growth means nurturing these linkages. Planning must be for the district as a whole, not for just its rural components or its urban enclaves.

We must, of course, build the local-level planning capabilities of the rural Panchayats, the Nagar Panchayats and the urban local bodies. We must also build structures that enable them to interact. The device resorted to by States like Maharashtra, Gujarat and West Bengal has been to set up district planning bodies with representation from the urban and rural local bodies under the chairmanship of a Minister nominated by the State Government. I am not sure that this is an entirely satisfactory arrangement. It leaches the elected representatives of the Panchayats and urban bodies of real responsibility and entrusts too much authority to outside agencies. A happier solution might be to co-ordinate the urban and rural plans in the Zila Parishad and to inject the vital component of the urban-rural interface. The draft district plan could be discussed, debated and passed by a District Assembly composed of all the elected members of the rural and urban bodies. Such a district plan would become a key input in the planning process at higher levels. For districts which are wholly or very largely urban, the planning function might best vest in the Metropolitan Regional Planning Authority. I invite your views on these points.

The British were not concerned with development. Not surprisingly, therefore, the municipal bodies they established have seen themselves primarily as organisations for the supply of civic amenities, not as instruments of development. On the other hand, Panditji instituted Panchayati Raj primarily as an instrument of development. It has, therefore, been relatively easy to provide in the Constitution (64th) Amendment Bill for planning and the implementation of development schemes to be entrusted to the Panchayats. A bold initiative is needed in regard to the development role of urban local bodies. Of course, these development functions would, in some ways, be different from the development functions of the rural Panchayat. In the transitional phase, the development functions of the urban bodies would relate very closely to those of the rural Panchayats. As the settlement grows larger and somewhat removed from its rural setting, its development concerns will progressively change and its links with the rural hinterland undergo a qualitative transformation. But at every stage, up to and including its becoming a metropolitan area, municipal bodies must see themselves as not only supplying civic amenities but also undertaking a developmental role.

Because traditionally municipal bodies did not have a develop-mental role and because their finances were not expanded to keep pace with the large capital investments and the sophisticated technology needed to provide the required civic infrastructure, a whole crop of specialised bureaucratic and technical bodies has mushroomed in urban India, outside the framework of the elected municipalities. These specialised bodies include City Development Authorities, City Improvement Trusts, Water and Sewerage Boards, Industrial Development Authorities and even Town Planning agencies. In regard to Panchayati Raj Institutions, it has been proposed that all development agencies be brought within the purview of the elected Panchayats. Would it not be appropriate to similarly bring all specialised urban bodies under the aegis of elected local authorities?

A curious and telling feature of the British-conceived distinction between urban and rural India was the assumption that civic amenities are needed by the towns people but not really required by rural folk. Today, the demand for civic amenities in rural India is no different from that of urban India. Water supply, sewerage, housing, proper communications, telecommunications—all these and more are sought with as much keenness in the rural areas as in the urban. Indeed, a substantial part of the explanation for the emigration of people from the villages to the towns is provided by the urge for these civic amenities. The cruel paradox is that, although a citizen of an urban settlement is, by law, entitled to these amenities, the resources of municipalities are so strained that most urban citizens do not get what they are entitled to, and what they do get is of indifferent quality and worse.

Confronted with an urban influx far larger than they can cope with, the response of the municipalities had been to whisk away the unwanted immigrant or pretend that he does not exist by declaring him unauthorised and irregular. At this point steps in the slum bully, who provides protection of a kind and amenities of an order but, in exchange, hijacks the unauthorised slum into the murky mazes of the underworld.

We have to have a more rational way of regulating the flow of people from rural to urban areas. There is a need to strike a balance between the retention of talent in our villages and the dynamising of our urban settlements through new enterprise. The right balance can be struck only when we break away from the colonial pattern. We must ensure civic amenities through Panchayats in rural India and development functions through municipalities in urban India. Of course, there may be some differentiation in the nature of the civic amenities provided, especially as regards the kind of technology required to provide that amenity. Similarly, the development tasks required of a Panchayat would not be quite the same as in urban settlements.

In the Eleventh Schedule attached to the Constitution Amendment Bill, we have, in an illustrative manner, listed some of the municipal functions and development duties which should devolve on the Panchayats. A similar list would be required for the Twelfth Schedule to determine the civic duties and municipal responsibilities of urban settlements. The transitional structure, which deals with the phased transformation from rural to urban settlements, would presumably operate on both the Eleventh and the Twelfth Schedules, thus ensuring the continuum from the remotest hamlet to the largest metropolis.

In considering the structure of local self-government most suited to urban India, we are faced with a conundrum which we must resolve. At present, the size of our corporation wards is so large, averaging thirty thousand voters or more, that there is little personal contact between the individual voter and his representative. At this echelon itself, the power-broker insinuates himself to guard the doors of access to the elected corporator. An obvious answer to the problem might be to reduce the size of each ward. But, if that is done, the number of Corporators which, at present, already runs to nearly a hundred and fifty would have to be vastly expanded to five hundred or more, rendering the Corporations quite unviable and totally unwieldy. Even as it is, compared to a *Panch* whose voice counts for a fifth or at least a tenth of the total voice of the Panchayat, the urban corporator's voice is only one in 150. Thus, yet another echelon is provided for the power-broker to insinuate himself.

The solution to the problem might lie in multi-tier local self-government. The first tier should appropriately be the neighbourhood Panchayat. The neighbourhood Panchayat, whether in a Nagar Panchayat or in a Municipality or in a Corporation, should not exceed a population of, say, ten to twenty thousand. That way each group of five hundred to a thousand voters would have a representative in the neighbourhood Panchayat, and the representative would count among the ten or so members constituting the neighbourhood Panchayat. Thus would begin the process of eliminating the power-broker between the voter and his representative, as also between the representative and the decision-making authority.

In Nagar Panchayats and Municipalities, a second tier at town level might suffice. But in metropolitan areas, with a population of, say, three hundred thousand and above, perhaps it would be useful to institute an intermediate tier. This intermediate tier would correspond to the Borough Council and could have functions similar to the administrative zones which already exist in cities like Bombay and Delhi.

A major objection to multi-tier local self-government is the explosion in establishment charges that this would involve. If every neighbourhood Panchayat were to set itself up as a mini-Municipality, there would, of course, be a vast increase of infructuous expenditure of offices, furnishing, staff, transport and telephones. But if the staffing pattern of the neighbourhood Panchayat were limited to the pattern and practice for village

Panchayats, and if service in the neighbourhood Panchayat were conceived in the Gandhian spirit of voluntary service, there could be strict control over the additional expenditure involved. We could easily establish a ceiling on establishment charges and insist that any additional expenditure on establishment must be raised by the neighbourhood Panchayat itself. Even that might not be necessary if members of neighbourhood Panchayats were to obey Mahatma Gandhi's injunction. As Gandhiji wrote in an article in *Young India* in 1929: "I think it is a rare privilege for a person to find himself in the position of a municipal councillor. But the indispensable condition of privilege is that Municipal Councillors dare not approach their office for interested or self-motives. They must approach their sacred task in a spirit of service."

I would invite your views on the principle of multi-tier local self-government, the attendant problems and potentialities, and the flexibility that might be built into the Constitutional provisions on the subject.

I now turn to the vexed problem of the finances of urban bodies. Almost everywhere in the country, municipal finances are in an unmitigated mess. Nothing would be more disastrous than devolving political power to elected members of Municipalities without simultaneously devolving fiscal responsibility on them. Where are the finances for sound municipal administration to come from? Central taxation and State taxation have already virtually reached the limits of possibility. There are not many more sources left to tap. There is not much more that can be squeezed out of the system. Of course, there must be devolution of funds along with devolution of functions from State Governments to urban local bodies. There must also be devolution of funds from Central revenues to the urban bodies, either through the agency of the State Governments or in some special cases, even directly to the municipal bodies. But beyond that, urban bodies must be endowed with the power, and, the responsibility and the incentive to seek their own sources of finance. There is the capital market to which they may seek access. We would like to strengthen the access of municipalities to the commercial banking network. We have in mind a refinancing body for urban areas similar to the National Bank for Agriculture and Rural Development (NABARD) which has functioned with great success in rural India.

But, over and above all these techniques, the essence of the matter is the devolution of fiscal powers to the urban bodies, which will empower and entrust to them the responsibility to themselves raise a substantial proportion of the resources they require. Provided the urban local bodies are allowed and encouraged to establish a nexus between the funds they raise and the funds they spend, sweetened by the incentive of matching grants, there will be every possibility of their putting in the required effort to ensure sound finance.

The reality of urban poverty is inescapable. We have Centrally-sponsored schemes of poverty alleviation in rural areas. A major objective of these schemes is to stem the flow of the rural needy from rural India to the urban dream that so quickly turns into the urban nightmare. There is the apprehension that the launching of poverty alleviation schemes in urban India might only encourage further the flow of the rural needy into urban slums. At the same time, it is inhuman to do nothing about the daily tragedy of urban poverty. It is important also to help the human resources of urban India realise their full economic potential. We are working on a carefully structured system of urban poverty alleviation programmes which would reach out to the poor of urban India without provoking a flood into our towns and cities of the rural needy.

I am particularly concerned about how the district and mofussil bureaucracy will react to the changes we are contemplating. I was encouraged to see that the municipal officers we met did not feel threatened by the assurance of democracy and political authority to the municipal bodies with which they are associated. On the contrary, there was unanimous approbation for our initiative. Nevertheless, I hope Chief Ministers will pay particular attention to the need for training and orientation programmes to assist the bureaucracy in effecting a smooth transition to the new system.

The agenda papers before you set out in detail the points on which we seek your guidance. In addition to the issues listed there, I would like your advice on two additional points.

One, do municipal bodies require a constabulary or peace force of their own which they can deploy for the law and order questions that attach to the discharge of municipal functions, such as the removal of encroachments? Second, should municipal bodies be encouraged to recruit their own staff or should there be, at the higher echelons, a State-wide or even All-India Service of Municipal and Panchayat Officers?

In bringing power to the people of urban India as we have sought to do through the Panchayati Raj Bill for rural India, we have been firm on principles but flexible on approaches.

We cannot be shaken from our resolve to give Constitutional sanctity to local self-government in both urban and rural areas. We cannot be shaken from our resolve to ensure through the Constitution that elections to local bodies will be held regularly. We cannot be shaken from our resolve that there shall be reservations for Scheduled Castes and Scheduled Tribes in proportion to their population, and that women will be assured of 30 per cent of seats in all local bodies. We also cannot be shaken from our resolve to ensure Constitutional authority for the devolution of administrative powers and real fiscal responsibility to these bodies. For the rest, we are open-minded.

We are amending the Constitution not because we wish to infringe States' rights but because local self-government requires the same Constitutional sanctity as the Constitution assures to the Union Parliament and to the State Assemblies. This is not a dispute over the Centre's jurisdiction and the rights of the States, as is sought to be made out in certain quarters. The opposition to guaranteeing power to the people is being dressed up in bogus Constitutional arguments. This is not an issue for confrontation between the Centre and the States. This is an issue for confrontation between the people and the vested interests. This is an issue between our commitment to power to the people and the determination of the feudal and capitalist interests to retain their power.

We have demonstrated through the Panchayati Raj Bill that we are scrupulously adhering to the basic structure of the Constitution. We have been most solicitous of the rights and privileges which the Constitution confers upon the States. We have not touched Entry 5 of the State List. We have not sought to transfer local self-government from the State list to the Concurrent List or the Central List. We have not attempted any Central municipal legislation on the subject. The process of implementing the Constitutional provisions rests with the State Legislatures and the State Government. The Panchayati Raj Bill seeks only to set the Constitutional stage for action by State authorities. Our proposed Bill on the urban local bodies will attempt no more.

The people are with us. Those who oppose us will have to reckon with the people.

One last word. Should we not consider using the word "Panchayats" not only for institutions of rural local self-government but also as the specifically Indian word for all forms of local self-government, both in rural and in urban India? For as Gandhiji said: "Panchayat has an ancient flavour; it is a good word".

10

Maximum Democracy and Maximum Devolution

The House would recall that when I introduced the Constitution (64th Amendment) Bill on the 15th May, I had said that Government intended to bring forward in the Monsoon Session major legislation relating to the urban local bodies. We are now fulfilling that commitment.

Already, in common parlance, the Bill I introduced in the last session is called the Panchayati Raj Bill and this, the Nagarpalika Bill. Allow me, Sir, to use these familiar names rather than the somewhat ponderous official titles.

The Nagarpalika Bill supplements the Panchayati Raj Bill. The theme of this Bill is the same as that of the other: Constitutional sanction for maximum democracy and maximum devolution. Even as we see the strengthening of the Panchayati Raj System as the key to eliminating the power-brokers from the life of rural India, so do we see this Bill as the key instrument for reducing and eventually eliminating the role of the power-brokers in urban India. We seek through these Bills to vest power in the only place where power rightfully belongs in a democracy in the hands of the people.

In the past few days, we have been sad witnesses to the gravest assault on democracy since the founding of our Republic: the abandonment of the Lok Sabha by a section of the elected representatives of the people. In the last general elections, the people gave the Congress an overwhelming mandate to govern the country for five years. In the same elections, they returned a few Opposition members to occupy the Opposition Benches for the same five years. The Members of the Opposition were elected to fulfil the vital democratic function of contesting the Government and its policies right here on the floor of this House, not in the streets or in the columns of newspapers. We respect those democratic and independent-minded members of the Opposition who are here with us today to democratically debate the issues of fundamental national importance which I shall be raising. By the same token, we must deplore the behaviour of those other Members of the Opposition who have simply run away from this highest forum of democratic dialogue. They have abused this noble institution to which they were elected. They have violated their mandate. They have betrayed their constituents. They have eroded democracy itself. Why have they tried to destroy democracy in Parliament? I have no doubt that it is primarily because they could not bear to see democracy devolved to the people. Had they stayed, they would have been exposed. They have fled. It has only exposed them sooner. A stern reckoning awaits them.

The people will, of course, consign to the dustbin of history of those who have resigned the seats to which they were elected in 1984. Yet, this only increases the responsibility of those of us who have remained in this House to strengthen the foundations of our democracy.

Democracy in Parliament and in the State Legislatures remains fragile so long as the roots of our democracy do not reach down to the villages and *mohalla* where the people live. Our Constitution detailed the provisions for democracy in Parliament and in the State Legislatures. Therefore, democracy in these institutions has survived every vicissitude and flourished. However, our Constitution did not make democracy in local self-government a Constitutional obligation. And so democracy in the Panchayats and Nagarpālika has withered at the roots.

With these two Bills, we shall ensure that while India lives, democracy at the grassroots lives. No longer will democracy in local self-government be a passing political pastime. Through these bills, democracy in local self-government becomes a solemn Constitutional obligation, an obligation that can neither be suborned nor flouted for reasons of expediency or indifference.

We wanted to come to this house only after consulting all the Chief Ministers. Tragically, but in keeping with their penchant to avoid democratic discussions, all but two of the non-Congress Chief Ministers stayed away from the discussions. Many of them refused to let the elected representatives of their parties participate in the Nagarpalika *Sammelans* and I believe one of them has dismissed some of those who participated in those discussions. They denied permission to their Municipal officers to attend the Conference of Municipal Officers called by the Ministry of Urban Development. We have done our best. We have done all we can to involve them in a nation-wide debate. They say there must be consensus before the Constitution is amended, but refuse to come for a discussion. How can a consensus be forged without dialogue? Their non-cooperation notwithstanding, we come to Parliament at the end of the widest and most intensive series of consultations undertaken in the history of Independent India. I have personally interacted with upward of 25,000 knowledgeable, experienced persons, most of whom are elected representatives of the people, before coming to this House with the Panchayati Raj and Nagarpalika Bills.

We have often stressed that this is not a Centre-State issue. Why should the Constitutional enshrinement of democracy in the Panchayats and the Nagarpalikas be a bone of contention between the Centre and the States? Why must regular elections, the end of arbitrary suspensions, and restitution within six months of the people's will be a matter of dispute between the Centre and the State? Why should reservations for the Scheduled Castes and the Scheduled Tribes and women be a matter of confrontation between the Centre and the State? There is in fact no contention between us, at the Centre, and the Government in the States. There is contention only between those of us who wish to empower the people and those political forces who wish to see power retained in the hands of feudal oligarchies and the couerie of power brokers they represent.

Far from encroaching on States' rights, we have displayed the utmost sensitivity to the structure of Centre-State relationships built through the Constitution. Entry Five of the State List remains untouched. The sovereignty of State Legislatures remains undiminished. We are amending the Constitution, not drafting municipal law on a State subject. What is being taken away is the right to ignore the people. What is being removed is the right to flout the people's will. What is being ended is the reign of the power brokers. It is not a question of the Centre's rights *versus* the States' rights. It is a question of the people's rights.

In according Constitutional status to the Nagarpalikas, we are but responding to the joint resolution passed by the Central Council of Local Self-government and the All-India Council of Mayors pleading for the conferment of Constitutional status on the urban local bodies. In both these bodies were represented Ministers, Mayors and other elected representatives of the Opposition parties, including political parties represented in this House today and those that have run away. Ranging from the CPI(M) to the BJP, and taking in much that lies in between, official spokesmen of all these parties have again and again asked for Constitutional recognition for the Nagarpalikas.

As recently as in their representation to the National Commission on Urbanization, the Calcutta Corporation, headed by a CPI(M) Mayor, argued that a country "wedded to grassroots-level democracy must bless its local institutions with a Constitutional status." They went on to say: "This bold initiative would become much more meaningful if the roles, functions, responsibilities (fiscal and other) and obligations of various levels of government are Constitutionally defined."

And I cannot resist quoting also their categorical conclusion that urban problems cannot be solved without giving "local governments their rightful place in the country's Constitutional framework, itself."

What has happened to change their minds? Let me phrase the question in a different way: What has happened—to change their principles? Is it that they are getting too used to the company of those with diametrically opposed ideologies and those with no principle or ideology at all?

We have heard the argument that there is no need for a Constitutional Amendment to bring democracy to the grassroots and endow power to the people. It has been argued that what is needed is political will. I respectfully submit, that it takes more political will to amend the Constitution than it does to pass a municipal law. I would also respectfully submit, that our Constitutional Amendment creates the necessary political will where that will does not exist. No party in India can claim an unblemished record in local self-government. Equally, there is no major political party in India which has not something to its credit in regard to local self-government. There are some Congress Governments that have done better than others. Equally, there are Opposition-run Governments which have done sometimes better than others, sometimes worse, indeed sometimes better than their own past record, while sometimes falling short of their past achievement. Our approach to the Panchayati Raj and Nagarpalika Bills has been non-partisan. We have drawn from the experience of all. We are beholden to all. We now bring forward a Bill which makes democratic decentralization to the Nagarpalikas, a keystone of the country's Constitutional arch.

Having discovered that there is an irresistible groundswell of popular support for Panchayati Raj and Nagarpalika Bills, one Opposition party has now come up with an alternative proposal for a Constitutional Amendment. The proper forum to table such amendments would be the floor of this House. But since the Party mainly responsible for these alternative proposals has fled from its democratic responsibilities, their proposals cannot even be considered. Let us see what happens in the other House where, in glaring contrast to their behaviour here, they cling like limpets to their seats.

Then there are the purists of the Opposition who say that, in no circumstances, will they have any truck with Constitutional provisions for local self-government. Their purity is, however, called into question when one discovers that, as recently as at the February 1989 Joint Meeting of the Central Council for Local Government and the All-India Council of Mayors, the delegations of the Telugu Desam Government of Andhra Pradesh, the Left Front Government of Kerala, and the CPI(M) Mayor of Calcutta, leading a delegation of the Left Front Government of West Bengal, were all party to a resolution which demanded a Constitutional amendment in relation to the Nagarpalikas.

There are yet other constituents of the National Front or, should I say the National Front? Who demanded at the 11th Joint Meeting a uniform statute for all Nagarpalikas in the country. How can these be a uniform statute without a Constitutional Amendment? And even assuming for a moment that this is achieved by some legal legerdemain, the essential difference between a Constitutional Amendment and a Municipal statute remains. The consequences of a Constitutional Amendment are ineluctable. Our proposals would enshrine democracy in the local bodies in the most sacred basis of our modern nationhood. In contrast, any model Bill will have no binding significance for State Legislatures and no guarantee of outlasting changes of party or personality. If we really want democracy and devolution in the Nagarpalikas, there is no alternative to the kind of Constitutional amendments we propose.

The starting point of the Nagarpalika Bill is the recognition that those who live in the urban settlements are entitled to the same democratic rights and the same rights and responsibilities for development, as we seek to confer on rural India through the Panchayati Raj Bill.

Already, a quarter of our population lives in urban India. The proportion will rise to a third by the turn of the century and cross the half-way mark within a few decades thereafter. This major demographic trend needs not only to be recognised but also encouraged. What has gone wrong with our pattern of urbanization is not that there is too fast and furious a flood of people into towns and cities, as that the pattern of urbanization is skewed. It is the larger metropolitan cities that are attracting the bulk of those coming in from the rural areas. This severely strains the resources of the larger cities without conferring any real benefit on the rural areas from where the new entrants have come. What we need is a rational pattern of urbanization. We need to see small and large towns growing in every district, drawing the bulk of their population from the surrounding rural hinterland. That way the talent and enterprise of the people will remain, to a large extent, within the district. Urbanization will be related to rural requirements. Urban settlements will cease to be isolated compartments.

It is the compartmentalization of India into rigidly separated rural and urban settlements that has been the worst legacy of the colonial system of local self-government. When, 107 years ago, the British introduced their system of urban local self-government, the urban settlements of India had a very different role to play to the one we now envisage for them. The colonial government of the time saw the urban settlements of India as enclaves where they could hide themselves comfortably from the surrounding reality. They assumed that drains and drinking water, street lighting and street cleaning were needed only for themselves and their hangers-on. It was assumed that civic amenities are not for rural India.

Four decades into Independence, the reality has changed but the shell remains much the same. The law makes it obligatory to provide civic amenities for all recognized urban settlements, but the strained resources of the urban local bodies make it almost impossible for them to meet their legal obligations. On the other hand, the inhabitants of rural India are demanding rightly that they too be given civic amenities, and-rightly-they are, increasingly, receiving their due.

We have to get out of the colonial categorization of India into separate rural and urban boxes. We have to replace the compartmentalization of rural and urban India by a rural-urban continuum, which threads the farthest rural hamlet to the largest megapolis in a *rudrakshamala* of democracy and devolution.

Secondly, in the colonial system of Municipal administration there was no place for development planning and no role for development activities. Then Panditji introduced Panchayati

Raj to fill the rural vacuum left by the colonial legacy, he envisaged the institutions of Panchayati Raj as a crucial instrument of development. Although, over the years, the Panchayati Raj Institutions have decayed, they have remained, in concept at least, a prime instrument of development. In contrast, the Municipal bodies have withered but assumed no developmental role. The development of India is not possible without planning for development in our urban settlements as much as in our rural settlements. Indeed, planning at the crucial interface between the rural hinterland and the urban settlement will be the chief progenitor of accelerated growth.

Accordingly, the first chapter of the Bill we have tabled deals with settlements in transition from rural to urban.

As it is, such settlements constitute the single largest category of settlements beyond the rural village. The present tendency, in most parts of the country, is to classify such settlements as urban and take them entirely out of the purview of the rural-urban interface. We propose that, instead of a proliferation of non-viable urban local bodies at this end of the spectrum, Local Self-Government in the Nagar Panchayats partake of the flavour of both rural administration and urban administration. This is emphasised in the very name suggested for these bodies,, Nagar Panchayats, that is the simultaneous recognition of the urban character of such a settlement and its continuing link with the rural countryside. More to the point, the powers and responsibilities devolved on Nagar Panchayats draw both from the rural list and the urban list. Planning undertaken by Nagar Panchayats will marry the requirements of the rural hinterland to activity that can best be undertaken in the transitional settlement. The recognition and encouragement of Nagar Panchayats will draw away from the land, the populations that the village cannot support while retaining within the locality, for the common benefit of the rural hinterland and the urbanising settlement, the talent and enterprise of those willing to undertake the risk and the adventure of uprooting themselves from their ancestral villages. Instead of being hollow symbols of a false prestige, as the smaller Municipalities regrettably are at present, the Nagar

Panchayats will become the focal point of the dynamics of development.

We would hope that in every district, one or some of the Nagar Panchayats will grow into a town worthy of a Nagarpalika. It is by the even spread of towns around the country that we will take the pressure off the large metropolises as well as off the land. It is in the spread of such settlements that we seek a rationalization of the pattern of urbanization. It is also these settlements that will, progressively and in phases, serve as the foci for industrial growth centres. Thus, we bring together the recommendations of the National Commission on Urbanization and our scheme of growth centres. Let us now see how decentralized democracy in the Nagarpalikas compares with decentralized democracy in the Panchayats.

Democracy in village Panchayats has two distinctive characteristics. First, the individual voter has a close, personal relationship and ready access to the elected representative because, on an average, each *Panch* represents between 100 and 500 voters. Second, each *Panch* has a voice which counts a great deal in the Panchayat. It is the combination of these two factors the personal contact between the voters and the elected representatives and the importance of the elected representatives in the elected body which is the first essential step towards eliminating the power-broker from the polity.

In contrast to the three levels of Panchayati Raj—the village, the block, and the district—we have so far only had single-tier Municipal administration. This works fairly satisfactorily in smaller towns because the wards are small and these Municipal Council compact. However, as the town grows larger, the distance between the voter and his representative increases, and the number of members of the Municipality also tends to increase. By the time towns grow into cities, and cities into metropolises, the median size of the ward expands to 30,000 and more, extending, in the case of one Delhi ward, even to two lakhs and above. The membership of the Corporation also expands to nearly one hundred and fifty members.

To bring democracy in urban settlements closer to the people in the *mohallas* and the neighbourhoods where they live, the Nagarpalika Bill proposes two innovations. These innovations are by no means a radical new departure. They build upon existing informal arrangements and administrative structures.

In all urban settlements, with a population of a lakh or more—we propose the Constitution, by direct election, of Wards Committees, to whom the Municipality will devolve local powers and local responsibilities, and such finances as are required to carry out their assigned tasks. We leave it to State Legislatures to determine the territorial area and size of population which will be served by a Wards Committee. We would hope the jurisdiction of a Committee would be sufficiently compact to give citizens a sense of personal involvement in the affairs of their neighbourhood and ready access to the elected representatives to deal with their ward-level problems. The Ward Councillor will be a member of the Wards Committee of his area and will constitute the link between the Ward and the Municipality.

In cities with a population above three lakhs, we propose that the chairpersons of the Wards Committees be constituted into a Zonal Committee. The determination of the territorial area and size of population falling within a Zonal Committee is left to the State Legislatures to decide. Powers, responsibilities and finances will devolve to the Zonal Committee from the Municipal Corporation.

A great advantage of the introduction of a two-tier system of municipal administration in the larger Municipal Councils, and of a three-tier system of municipal administration in Municipal Corporation, is that it will leave Councillors and Corporators free to deal with city-level issues, with matters of policy such as city-wide infrastructure, overall economic and social development, linkages with neighbouring Municipalities and economic interaction with the district as a whole.

Hitherto, the absence of effective, representative local self-government has introduced a glaring distortion in our system. If a drain in a *mohalla* gets blocked, the Ward Councillor, the President of the Municipality, the MLA, the MP and the local Minister are all together approached to get the drain unblocked.

Sometimes the unblocking of the drain even requires the intervention of the Prime Minister.

The removal of such distortions requires a systemic change so that each level focuses on its level of responsibility.

The establishment of Wards Committees will give the people of the *mohalla* or *para*, the locality or neighbourhood, a sense of personal involvement in their civic affairs. It will afford an opportunity for public-spirited citizens to serve their locality. It will help focus attention on how the people themselves view their problems and the solutions they suggest. It will help mobilise local participation and local resources for local development. It will give voluntary organisations a neighbourhood forum in which to share ideas and explore the scope for citizen action. The city will then truly belong to the people.

The importance of this in the poorer parts of the city cannot be overemphasised. Today, the unrecognised and unwanted are left uncared for. They huddle together in festering slums. They are unrecognised because they are unauthorised. They wait in dread of the moment when they will be uprooted. Uprooted, they settle themselves elsewhere, for settle somewhere they must. That they are unauthorised does not mean they do not exist. They do and for their protection they turn to the slum bully, who terrorises them into submission but in exchange, offers a measure of protection. The children of the unwanted are then sucked into the underworld. The Wards Committees offer these unfortunates a new hope of a new dawn. The *mohalla* can begin looking after its own. The elected representatives of the *mohalla* will look after the interests of the *mohalla*. The *mohalla* can cease being at the mercy of others. The slum bully will give way to the *mohalla* Panchayat, that is, the Wards Committee.

We have assured the involvement of the Ward Councillor or Corporator in the work of the Wards Committee. This will help him keep in close touch with locality-level problems but, at the same time, free him to consider larger questions of policy.

The country has enthusiastically welcomed the assurance of regular, periodic elections to the Panchayats every five years. Through this Bill, we seek to extend this provision to the

Nagarpalikas. The country has also greatly welcomed the proposal to reconstitute dissolved Panchayats within six months by direct election. We extend this provision too, through this Bill, to the Nagarpalikas.

Social justice demands representation for the Scheduled Castes and the Scheduled Tribes in proportion to their population. We have assured this in the Panchayats. We assure this too in the Nagarpalikas.

There is no section of our society more oppressed, more exploited and more neglected than women in every segment, class or community, women suffer all the disabilities inflicted on that group and, in addition, suffer also the consequences of gender discrimination. Yet, their contribution to economic life, social well-being, cultural continuity and ethical standards is far great than their share of the population. We must make a determined beginning to bring women into the mainstream of local self-government. It is proposed to extend reservations for women to Nagarpalikas on the same pattern as has been envisaged in the Panchayats.

I now turn to the functions of urban local bodies. The traditional civic functions of Municipalities are well-known and well-understood, if not always well-implemented. We would like to see the Nagarpalikas go beyond the mere provision of civic amenities. They should be empowered to play a crucial role in the preparation of plans for local development and in the implementation of development projects and programmes, including specially conceived programmes for urban poverty alleviation.

That is the only way of involving people in their own development and ending the *mai-baap* syndrome. Real responsibility will foster realistic expectations, and an understanding at the grassroots level of resource constraints Nagarpalika members, and those who elect them, must learn the necessity of choosing between alternative options, and the need to mobilise additional resources to meet additional demands. At the same time, the people's involvement in the planning process will lead to plans which respond to local needs and local desires. Planning should not be the unravelling of some bureaucratic fantasy about what is good for the people. It is for the people to themselves decide what is good for them.

I would like to particularly emphasise that the Nagarpalika Bill stresses, as does the Panchayati Raj Bill, that planning by local bodies should deal not only with economic development but also with social justice. This means that no plan for economic development drawn up by any local body will be valid unless its social justice component has been specifically spelt out in the plan. Thus, social justice is not left as an adjunct to the planning process but made an integral part of it.

Planning without resources is an invitation to irresponsibility. On the other hand, planning based on a clear idea of the magnitude of available resources, and anchored, to the extent possible, in self-generated resources is the *sine qua non* of responsible planning. We propose that a Finance Commission be constituted in every State to review Municipal finances and recommend principles on the basis of which the sound finance of the Nagarpalikas can be assured. As in the case of Panchayati Raj Institutions, this would involve the earmarking of certain taxes for assignment to, or appropriation by, the Nagarpalikas, in addition to grants-in-aid. It is our hope that Finance Commissions would see their way to progressively devolving to the Nagarpalikas fiscal responsibility for the appropriation of the revenues of more and more taxes, duties, tolls and fees, because it is when a nexus is established between revenues raised and revenues spent that local bodies are best able to exercise fiscal responsibilities. We recognise, of course, that no Nagarpalika will be able to survive on its self-generated resources alone. A system of incentive grants is essential to provide an additional stimulus for fiscal responsibility and financial self-reliance.

There is scope for the Nagarpalikas to go much further in looking for resources for local development. They must be encouraged to seek access to the capital market, of course keeping in mind their capacity to service the Municipal debt. There is need for specialised financial institutions to deal with Municipalities and urban development, in particular, housing. There is need also for a refinance body similar to the National

Bank for Rural and Agricultural Development (NABARD). We are making a study of these possibilities.

The Panchayati Raj Bill seeks to devolve powers and responsibilities for planning to Panchayati Raj Institutions. The Nagarpalika Bill does the same for the Nagarpalikas. Any district is, however, a composite of its Panchayats and its Nagarpalikas. It is, therefore, essential to have a mechanism for consolidating and harmonising the plans prepared by different Panchayats and Nagarpalikas, preparatory to drafting a development plan for the district as a whole.

This brings us back to our running theme of the rural-urban continuum. Colonialism created the artificial rural-urban divide. Democracy and devolution must restore the interaction of rural and urban settlements so that the district as a whole prospers. With planning in the towns fostering in the countryside, more remunerative cropping patterns, higher agricultural productivity, greater incomes and larger employment and, reciprocally, urban prosperity being accelerated by linkages with the rural economy and with other urban settlements in the district, we must create an awareness and a recognition of the advantages of the integrated development of the district as a whole.

It is, therefore, proposed that a joint Committee of the Nagarpalikas and Panchayats be established to undertake these tasks. The Committee will be elected by the members of the Zila Panchayat and the Nagarpalikas from amongst themselves in proportion to the ratio of the rural to the urban population. Reservations for the Scheduled Castes, Scheduled Tribes and women will be assured in the Committee. Thus, the district development plan will not only include the social justice component of the plans prepared by each Panchayat and Nagarpalika. It will be prepared and finalised only with the full participation of the Scheduled Caste and Scheduled Tribe representatives, in proportion to their population, and with women constituting 30 per cent of the membership of the committee.

For metropolitan areas, the Nagarpalika Bill proposes the establishment of a Committee to consolidate and harmonise the development plans of the Panchayats and Nagarpalikas comprised within the metropolitan area, as also to prepare the development plan for the metropolitan area as a whole. We have ensured popular representation in the Committee by providing that at least two-thirds of the members will be elected from and amongst the members of the Nagarpalikas and the chairpersons of the Panchayats falling within the metropolitan area. The remaining one-third could represent authorities with special interest in the metropolitan area as well as government representatives and persons of eminence.

In the course of the nation-wide debate that has followed the introduction of the Panchayati Raj Bill, apprehensions have been expressed about criminals and anti-social elements entering the body politic through the local bodies. Such apprehensions are not without foundation. We have had several instances in the past of persons who would be disqualified from standing for Assembly or Parliamentary elections, being able to contest local body elections. The Constitution affords protection against the entry of such persons into the Assemblies and Parliament. Its very silence on the subject of disqualifications for membership of the Panchayats and the Nagarpalikas has resulted in State legislation leaving wide open the lacunae and loopholes through which such undesirable elements have wormed their way into the local bodies. We are plugging the gap. The Bill before the House details the disqualifications for the Panchayats and the Nagarpalikas based upon the existing Constitutional provisions in regard to the Assemblies and Parliament, as well as disqualifications prescribed through legislation. The implication is that all the disqualifications we introduced through our amendment last December to the Representation of People's Act will also apply to candidates contesting elections to the Panchayats and the Nagarpalikas. Our Bill also opens the possibility for State Legislatures to introduce other disqualifications which may be necessitated by local conditions.

The Constitutional Amendments which I commend for your consideration constitute but the first stage of a process. The process must be carried forward to the second stage of State legislation and the third stage of executive implementation.

Many of the details of the new system can be settled only at these subsequent stages. Quite rightly, high importance is attached to such matters as the convening of Gram Sabhas to consider issues of importance, transparency in the proceedings of the Panchayats and the dissemination of public information about their decisions, the public notification of electoral rolls, and the public display of information about the implementation of programmes such as the Jawahar Rozgar Yojana, including details of the works undertaken, the expenditure made, and the names of beneficiaries. These are matters that cannot be dealt with in a Constitutional amendment but must be dealt with at later stages. State legislation, the rules made thereunder and the Government Orders issued will, we hope, not merely conform to the letter and spirit of these Amendments, but creatively interpret them to fulfil the high expectations our people have reposed in the rejuvenation and revitalization of the Panchayats and Nagarpalikas. It would be the responsibility of State Governments to undertake the required dispositions to bring within the purview of the elected authority, the district bureaucracy and official agencies operating in the district. The recruitment, training and orientation of the Government servants who will serve the local bodies is a State responsibility. It would be for the State Governments to ensure the proper staffing and the smooth flow of funds to finance the assigned tasks and devolve functions of the Panchayats and the Nagarpalikas. All these are tasks which call for close co-operation between the Union Government and the State Governments. Our co-operation is pledged. The people will not forgive the State Governments who fail to co-operate. So, our task does not end with the consideration and passage of these Bills. We would hope a vociferous public opinion and vigilant monitoring will ensure that our intentions are fully and faithfully realised.

The Constitution Amendment Bills, we bring before, this House by no means constitute the end of our grassroots revolution. We look forward, in the next Lok Sabha, to thoroughly revamping the cooperative movement which, in many sectors and many parts of the country, has run a ground on the shoals of upper-class domination, mismanagement, malfeasance and worse. We are also conscious of our work on the Panchayats being unfinished because we have not yet dealt with the Nyaya Panchayats. Equally, in urban India, we need to complement responsive administration with the quick delivery of justice. This work will be a major priority for our Government in the Ninth Lok Sabha.

This is a moment of history. This is a moment of revolution. The decisions we take will decisively determine the destiny of our democracy. We are here in this House by the will of our people. It is to the people that we shall return shortly to seek a renewal of our mandate. Five years ago, we had promised our people a radical restructuring of Government at the grassroots to make it more representative, more responsible and more responsive.

We are now on the threshold of the most significant systemic change to take place since the adoption of the Constitution 40 years ago.

With these two Bills, we redeem our pledge to our people. Power to the people. The people are with us.

11

Dimensions of Panchayati Raj and Nagarpalika Bills

I have been following with the closest interest this important debate on the Panchayati Raj and Nagarpalika Bills.

These Constitutional Amendments, which I had the honour to introduce at the last session, are of truly historic and revolutionary significance. It is, therefore, not surprising that the debate should have been sometimes stormy, sometimes incisive, sometimes reflective, but at all times lively. I wish to thank all members on both sides of the House for the important contributions they have made to this debate which is bound to adorn textbooks on Constitutional history for many years to come.

By and large, it appears to me, there is general acceptance of the need for maximum democracy and maximum devolution. What is disputed are matters of Constitutional jurisdiction, political propriety, electoral motivation and legislative detail. Allow me to deal with each of these apprehensions in turn.

It has now been well-established in both Houses that there can be no doubt about the Union Government's competence to introduce these Constitutional Amendments. We have displayed the utmost rectitude in not impinging upon the essential Constitutional relationship established between the Union and the States. Our basic aim is to secure Constitutional sanctity for democracy in the Panchayats and Nagarpalikas and devolution to them of adequate power and finances to ensure the people's participation in the development process.

First, we have left Entry Five of the State List exactly as it is and where it is. The competence of State legislatures to deal with all municipal legislation relating to rural and urban local bodies has not been tampered with in any way.

Second, care has been taken to so draft the Constitutional Amendments as to leave it entirely to State Legislatures to draft the law on the subject, and to State Governments to formulate and pass the necessary orders to realise the objectives of these Constitutional Amendments. The only point I would wish to stress is that all municipal laws have to conform to the provisions of the Constitution. These two Amendments, when passed, will set the Constitutional stage on the basis of which State Legislatures will undertake detailed legislation.

Third, it is erroneous and misleading today, as some members opposite have alleged, that what we have attempted to do is to draft detailed municipal legislation by the backdoor of detailed Constitutional Amendments. We have restricted ourselves to essential features such as regularity in elections and the forestalling of arbitrary and prolonged suspensions.

We have been asked why we have prescribed in such detail a common structure of Panchayats at village, intermediate and district levels, as also a common structure of Nagarpalikas for different sizes of population. The answer is simple.

A uniform structure means a uniform pattern and degree of democratic representation in the local bodies. Why should the pattern and degree of democracy differ from one part of the country to the other? We are, after all, one country. Another major objective we have in mind is to reduce the vast gap that now separates the voter from his representative. In a vast country like ours, there are at present no more than about five thousand five hundred persons—five thousand in the State Legislatures and around five hundred in Parliament—to directly represent 800 million people. The number of voters seeking the assistance of the elected representative is so large that there is no way the representative can really give his personal attention to his electorate as a whole. Also, it means the people have to approach their MLA, or even MP, to get grassroots problems attended to. The Panchayati Raj and Nagarpalika Bills will generate so many lakhs of elected grassroots representatives that the distance between the voter and his representative would be drastically reduced, the power-brokers would be driven from their perches, and grassroots problems would receive grassroots attention. There is no reason why these benefits should not reach the people in a more or less uniform manner throughout the country. That objective can only be secured by uniformity in the structure of local bodies.

The third point is, perhaps, of the greatest significance. We are determined to ensure just representation for the weaker sections of society through reservations in all our local bodies. The only way of ensuring uniformity in reservations is by ensuring a uniform structure of local government.

Let me give you an example to illustrate the complications that would have arisen if we had tried to secure a uniform system of reservations without having a uniform structure of local government. At present, in some States, including Congress-run Maharashtra and non-Congress-run West Bengal, the Panchayat Samiti is a body directly elected by the people at large.

In some other States, however, the Panchayat Samiti is not a directly elected body but a committee of the Chairmen of Village Panchayats. In a directly elected Panchayat Samiti it is entirely feasible to reserve seats for Scheduled Castes and Scheduled Tribes in proportion to their population, as also to reserve 30 per cent of the seats for women. If, however, the Panchayat Samiti is not a directly elected body but only a committee of the Chairmen of the Village Panchayats, how is one to secure proportionate representation for Scheduled Castes and Scheduled Tribes or 30 per cent reservation for women?

In prescribing a uniform structure of local government for the country as a whole, our aim is not to arbitrarily impose a uniform structure on a diverse country. It is only to ensure that there is uniformity of reservations throughout the country for the Scheduled Castes, the Scheduled Tribes and women. We are second to none in recognising the diversity of our country.

We are second to none in celebrating the variegated cultures of our country. We are second to none in being the most passionate advocates of our unity in diversity, in recognising and affirming that, in a country like India, the only unity that is possible is by a large-hearted acceptance of diversity. Respect for diversity means recognising that palm trees grow in some parts of the country and the chinar grows elsewhere. But what has this to do with the oppression of *Harijans* or *Adivasis* or discrimination against women? Surely, the ladies of Kerala deserve equal treatment in the Panchayats as the ladies of Kashmir, even as Scheduled Castes and Scheduled Tribes everywhere are entitled to equal representation. Diversity means respect for a *Carnatic Kriti* in Thanjavur, a *baul* in Bengal, a *dhrupad* in Gwalior and a *manganiar lok-geet* in Rajasthan. But does this mean reservations in Tamil Nadu should be different to reservations in Bengal?

That the *Adivasis* of Rajasthan should be treated differently to the *Adivasis* of Madhya Pradesh? That Scheduled Castes in one part of the country should get reservations in proportion to their population but be denied the same privilege in other parts of the country? To do this would be to make a farce of the noble precept of unity in diversity.

We celebrate the intellectual, spiritual and cultural diversity of our country. But, as I said a minute ago, we are one country. When it comes to oppression and discrimination, the people of India are united in demanding a uniform end to all oppression, all suppression, all social tyranny, all obsolete social mores. I repeat that it is to secure a uniform system of reservations that we were obliged to prescribe a uniform structure of local government.

I now turn to questions of political propriety which appear to have agitated the feelings of our friends opposite. We have been asked: how dare the Prime Minister interact directly with District Magistrates? I answer: what call has the Prime Minister of a country like India to remain as Prime Minister unless he feels at home in the humblest hut of the remotest village of our vast and varied country? I toured hundreds of villages. I spoke to countless people. There, in their hearths and homes, I experienced the cruelty of an unresponsive administration, the oppression of an administration without a heart, the callous lack of compassion that most of our people find at the hands of much of our administration. I then looked at the Administrators themselves—most of them dedicated young men and women, of extraordinarily high intelligence, deeply concerned about the people placed in their charge and yet, apparently, incapable of converting their enthusiasm and personal compassion into a responsive administration. I sought an answer to this riddle, a solution to this conundrum. That is how I decided to pose the question to the District Magistrates themselves. How could this possibly be wrong?

In any case, there was nothing clandestine about my encounters with District Magistrates. The first one was held at Bhopal. I invited Chief Minister Vora to join us-he accepted. The second one was held at Hyderabad. I invited Chief Minister N.T. Rama Rao to accompany me to the encounter. For reasons best known to him, he haughtily declined. I asked him once again at Hyderabad airport. He once again refused to come with me. How can the Opposition now turn around and say I went behind the backs of Chief Ministers to talk to District Magistrates?

When it came to meetings with village *pradhans* and *sarpanches*, Panchayat Samiti Chairmen and Presidents of Zila Parishads, we took care to seek the co-operation of at least two Opposition-run State Governments in holding these *Sammelans*. Chief Minister Jyoti Basu kindly agreed to co-operate and we held a most informative and useful *Sammelan* in Calcutta, in full view, I might add, of the representatives of that State's non-Congress Government. We were making arrangements with an Opposition-run Government for the South Zone *Sammelan* in Bangalore when that Government crumbled under the weight of its own inconsistencies. If the Janata Dal Government failed to host the South Zone *Sammelan* that was not on account of any failings on our part but only because of their own inability to hold out until the Panchayat representatives arrived!

We have consulted openly, frankly and freely with every echelon concerned: beginning with the common folk of our villages to whom I spoke; then the bureaucracy, including District Magistrates, Chief Secretaries and Secretaries to the Government of India; and then the Panchayat and Local Self-Government Ministers and Chief Ministers of States. It was never we who shied away from meeting them. Regrettably, however, some Opposition-run State Governments refused to send officials and even elected representatives to these encounters and then, in a shameful act of abnegation of governmental responsibility, failed to participate in the Conference of Chief Ministers which I called in early July.

We have come to this House, at the culmination of a process of open, transparent consultation without precedent in the history of independent India. The Amendments we present are the distilled essence of the views of thousands of elected local body representatives, hundreds of District Magistrates, scores of senior Government servants, and dozens of Ministers and Chief Ministers. There is no impropriety on our part. The only impropriety has lain in the discourtesy with which a well-intentioned invitation was turned down.

Much play has been made by the Opposition of the proximity of the forthcoming general elections to the important legislation which this House will shortly be voting upon. I do not quite understand the point at issue here. Is it not a fact that we were elected to govern and legislate for a five-year period? Should we stop governing and legislating only because elections are in the offing? It is the people who have given us this responsibility. It is to the people—and the people alone—that we are responsible. We reject this artful misinterpretation of Parliamentary practice that would require us to desist from legislation because of the proximity of the polls.

In any case, it was at the very beginning of our present term of office, in the first broadcast I made to the nation in January 1985, that I outlined the plan we had in mind to make our administration responsive to the people's needs. I raised these issues in my speech at the Congress Centenary in Bombay in December 1985. In August, 1986, this intention of Government was enshrined as the Twentieth Point of the

20-Point Programme under the rubric "Responsive Administration".

At that time, I must confess, we were in quest of managerial solutions to unresponsive administration. We were looking to a simplification of procedures, grievance redressal machinery, single-window clearances, computerisation and courtesy as the answers to the problem. As we went along, we discovered that a managerial solution would not do. What was needed was a systemic solution.

The Panchayati Raj and Nagarpalika Bills constitute the most significant systemic transformation in the governance of the Indian polity since the Constitution entered into force just under forty years ago. We learnt that a paternalistic administration cannot be a responsive administration. We learnt that a grassroots administration without political authority was like a meal without salt. We learnt that however well-intentioned our district bureaucracy might be, without effective elected authority the gap between the people and the bureaucracy could not be closed. We learnt that the vacuum created by the absence of local level political authority had spawned the power-brokers who occupy the gap between the people and their representatives in distant Vidhan Sabhas and the even more remote Parliament. We learnt that corruption could only be ended by giving power to the Panchayats and making Panchayats responsible to the people. We learnt that inefficiency could only be ended by entrusting the people at the grassroots with the responsibility for their own development. We learnt that callousness could only be ended by empowering the people to send their own representatives to institutions of local self-government, by empowering the people to reject those who betray their mandate.

The Panchayati Raj and Nagarpalika Bills are not only instruments for bringing democracy and devolution to every-*chaupal* and every *chabutra*, to every *angan* and every *dalan*. They are also a charter for ending bureaucratic oppression, technocratic tyranny, crass inefficiency, bribery, red-tapism, nepotism, corruption and the million other malfeasances that afflict the poor of our villages, towns and cities. The Bills are the warrant for ending the reign of the power-brokers, of the intermediaries whom Shakespeare called "the caterpillars of the commonwealth".

These Bills fill a yawning gap in the country's polity. They are the result of a process that was started in the immediate aftermath of our great electoral victory and has been carried forward in carefully considered stages till it has ripened for consideration by our august Houses of Parliament. There is nothing sudden or surprising about the timing of these Bills.

There is another point I would wish to stress. Elections come and go. The consequences of these Constitutional Amendments will far outlast the outcome of the forthcoming general elections. These Amendments will become a sacred obligation on all Governments, whether at the Centre or in the States, whether run by the Congress or any Opposition party. There is nothing gimmicky about our intentions. We are making democracy at the grassroots a solemn and ineluctable Constitutional obligation. Equally, we are making the devolution of administrative and financial powers to the local bodies an inescapable responsibility of all governments, now and in the future, here at the Centre and there in the States, a responsibility as much of Congress-run governments as of governments run by others. On election gimmick is a trick of the trade. A Constitutional Amendment is a solemn, long-term pledge. Ours is a pledge to the people. Those who thwart the people do so at grave risk to themselves. When the voter stands in the seclusion of the voting booth his hand will go down on the hand which clasps his as a friend.

I would now like to deal with some of the matters in detail touched upon by participants in this debate.

It has been alleged that Schedules Eleven and Twelve infringe in some manner upon the legislative sovereignty of the State Legislatures and the freedom of action of State Governments in regard to responsibilities assigned to them by the Constitution.

The confusion appears to arise out of confounding the legislative lists of the Seventh Schedule and the lists incorporated in the proposed Eleventh and Twelfth Schedules. The Union, State and Concurrent lists detailed in the Seventh Schedule deal with the respective legislative competence of the Union, the States, and the Union and States together. The Eleventh and Twelfth Schedules, on the other hand, constitute an illustrative listing of subjects in respect of which development programmes might be implemented by Panchayats and Nagarpalikas respectively. These are subjects regarding which understanding at the local level is likely to be much more profound than in some distant State Capital and where implementation by local elected bodies is likely to be much more responsive to articulated public need than the cold ministrations of official agencies. The Eleventh and Twelfth Schedules do not confer any legislative competence upon the local bodies. Nothing is taken away from the legislative competence of State Legislatures. All that is indicated by the Eleventh and Twelfth Schedules is the path along which effective devolution might be pursued to render the Panchayats and Nagarpalikas into vibrant, dynamic, meaningful institutions of local self-government.

It is explicitly stated in the Constitutional Amendments now before the House that it would be for State Legislatures to lay down the legislative parameters of devolution and for State Governments to give practical effect to those parameters. We recognise that the precise pattern of devolution might vary from State to State. We leave it to the good sense of our people to endorse or reject through their vote the degree and nature of devolution conferred upon the Panchayats and Nagarpalikas by different State Legislatures and State Governments. Those State Governments that live up to the expectations of the people will receive the endorsement of the people. Those who fail the people will receive the rejection they deserve. Our sanction is the people's vote. The only threat we hold out to State Governments is the threat of their being rejected at the poll by the people whose Constitutional rights they transgress, by the people who feel deprived of the opportunities opened to them by these Constitutional Amendments.

Surprisingly little has been said in this debate about the

heart of the Amendments, which is the provision for planning and implementation.

It is undeniable that our planning has become increasingly removed from the perceptions and aspirations of our people at the grassroots. Such district planning as is taking place is largely formalistic in nature, a putting together by bureaucrats and technocrats of what they perceive to be in the interests of the people. The people themselves are not consulted at all, or are consulted but perfunctorily. Through these Amendments, the primary responsibility for planning would devolve upon the Panchayats at every level and each tier of the Nagarpalikas. Each local community, whether in a small village covered by a Village Panchayat, or in a village turning into a town governed by a Nagar Panchayat, or in a town governed by a Municipal Council, or in a city governed by a Corporation, would prepare its own plan for its own development.

I would particularly draw the attention of the House to the wording of the relevant provision. It provides, in effect, for any plan for economic development to incorporate its social justice component. As it is, the provision for reservations ensures that the Panchayat or Nagarpalika undertaking the planning exercise will be adequately weighted with the weaker sections of society. That in itself will contribute to a heightened social consciousness in the preparation of plans. But these constitutional provisions go even further. They make the completion of any plan prepared by a Panchayat or Nagarpalika contingent upon the incorporation in the plan of its social justice component. In other words, whereas until now even in so progressive a State as Gujarat, which has pioneered the Social Justice Committees in Panchayats, social justice has been an adjunct to the planning process, these Constitutional Amendments make social justice an integral element of the planning process.

Plans prepared by Panchayats, Panchayat Samitis and Nagarpalikas will then be filtered upwards to the Zila Parishad for harmonising and consolidation by a Committee elected by members of the Zila Parishad and the Nagarpalikas. This Committee for district planning incorporates members of the

Scheduled Castes and Scheduled Tribes in proportion to their population in the district and reserve 30 per cent of the seats for women. Thus, the very composition of the District Planning Committee is such as to ensure the integration of social justice with economic planning in district plans. This holds true equally of the elected body being established for metropolitan planning.

These Constitutional Amendments presage an entirely new era in planning, not only in terms of detailed consultations with the grassroots, but also in terms of ensuring social justice as an integral component of the development process.

As regards implementation, there has been a half-hearted attempt by some members of the Opposition to raise a laugh by pointing to one lacuna or the other in the Eleventh and Twelfth Schedules. These digs would have a purpose if there had been any attempt to make Eleventh and Twelfth Schedules either comprehensive or obligatory. We have made it amply clear that these two Schedules are illustrative in nature, aimed at indicating practical ways in which the implementation of programmes and projects might be entrusted to elected local bodies instead of being carried out, as present, by cold, remote official agencies. It is by being held responsible for the implementation of programmes that local bodies will become truly responsible to the people. It is when representativeness is combined with responsibility that responsive administration follows.

Moreover, the location of the District Planning Committee in the Zila Parishad, and indeed its very creation, provide the first-ever platform of rural-urban interaction on development issues. This in itself will contribute to a higher awareness of various problems of social injustice and the remedial measures required to rectify them. Through the proposed Metropolitan Planning Authority, India becomes one of the first developing countries in the world to provide a platform for interaction between the State and the Central authorities and the elected representatives of urban and adjacent rural local bodies, thus integrating the demands of the social justice with the imperatives of economic growth.

We have left it to State legislatures and State Governments

to determine the precise contours of the responsibilities that will devolve on local bodies for the implementation of programmes. Some States will go further than others. Some variation in the degree and pattern of devolution would be justified and acceptable. But any State Government which transgresses the spirit of these Amendments will have to face the wrath of the people.

We, at the Centre, have made a beginning in trusting the local bodies to implement their own programmes. The Jawahar Rozgar Yojana and the Nehru Rozgar Yojana are the earnest of our commitment to placing responsibility for development administration squarely in the hands of the elected representatives of the people at the grassroots. No longer will the people have to run from one bureaucratic closed door to another, from one indifferent official to another. No longer will they have to bribe and cajole their way to securing their legitimate rights. We are bringing to an end the Kafkaesque nightmare through which the people at the grassroots have lived. Their problems will now be solved at their doorstep. Answerability will be within the very villages where they live. Accountability would be nailed to the Panchayat Ghar and the Nagarpalika. Truth will not be hidden in ever-more voluminous files and cupboards bursting at the seams, but will be revealed on the floor of the Panchayat Ghar and at the Village hustings, on the floor of the Town Hall and the hustings in every *mohalla*.

As regards the sound finances of the Panchayats and Nagarpalikas, we propose entrusting this responsibility to the Finance Commissions envisaged in the Constitutional Amendments. Here again, some of the comments made by members Opposite would appear to indicate that while they have glimpsed some of the parallel features between the Finance Commission established under Article 280 of the Constitution and the Finance Commissions proposed in the present Amendments, they have not comprehended the essential differences between the two. Whereas the Finance Commission established under Article 280 affects the actual allocation of resources between the Centre and the States, the Finance Commissions referred to in these Amendments would limit themselves to the principles on the basis of which allocations might be made between the States and the local bodies. The actual allocations will be made by the State Governments in the light of State legislation on the subject and the principles recommended by the Finance Commissions.

We, at the Centre, are undertaking an exercise to review Nagarpalika and Panchayat finances with a view to seeing what steps might be taken to augment the availability of financial resources for local self-government. We would hope State Governments, both those run by our party and those run by Opposition Parties under take a similar exercise in self-enlightenment.

The Constitutional Amendments entrust to the Comptroller and Auditor General (CAG) the responsibility for causing the accounts of the local bodies to be prepared and audited in such manner as he deems fit. Members Opposite appear to have jumped to the conclusion that this means dismantling the existing State machinery for the examination and auditing of local bodies accounts. In our view. unless the CAG, in his wisdom, deems otherwise, there would be no need to dismantle existing State machinery nor undertake any substantial augmentation of the staff in the CAG's office. What the CAG is being mandated to do is to examine existing procedures in different States for the preparation and audit of local bodies accounts and prescribe methods by which such accounts and auditing might be made stricter and less prone to abuse. There is no question of requiring the CAG to himself take over the direct responsibility for accounting and auditing. The State local fund auditing bodies would continue to exercise their functions, but under the overall guidance and direction of the Comptroller and Auditor General.

I now turn to the dust being raised by the Opposition over the role of the Election Commission. Here again, it is a total misreading of the Constitutional amendments to suggest that the existing machinery for the conduct of elections to local bodies would have to be dismantled. The Election Commission will conduct the elections through State Electoral officers and their staff. Also as elections are going to be regular, and arbitrary, prolonged suspensions are to be outlawed, it would be essential to further strengthen the existing machinery. The important change we are effecting is not in centralising the conduct of elections but in bringing the process of election to local bodies under the purview of the Election Commission.

In recent months, the burden of responsibility on the Election Commission has been considerably increased. Legislative amendments undertaken in respect of the Representation of the People Act and other legislation have greatly added to the workload of the Commission. The responsibilities envisaged for them under the Panchayati Raj and Nagarpalika Bills will further increase the Chief Election Commissioner's responsibilities.

We seek no confrontation on these Bills. In preparing these Bills, we have drawn upon the experience of all, of Congress States as much as of non-Congress States. We have freely and repeatedly acknowledged our debt to Opposition Governments, like those in West Bengal and Andhra Pradesh, and the earlier Janata Government in Karnataka, who have made innovative contributions to the improvement of Panchayati Raj in our country. Equally do we owe a debt of gratitude to the pioneering Congress stalwarts in Gujarat and Maharashtra who have the longest unbroken and unblemished record of Panchayati Raj in the country. There are negative lessons also to be learnt, as we have freely and fully admitted, from inadequate or insufficient Panchayati Raj and Nagarpalika administration in some non-Congress States as well as in some Congress States. There is no partisan politics in this. Our only interest is the national interest, the interests of development, the interests of the poor, the interests of the weak.

We admit also that the objectives we seek to achieve are objectives which, at various times in the past, have been espoused by Opposition Parties, ranging all across the spectrum from the Bharatiya Janata Party (and its forbears) to the two Communist Parties (and their forbears).

We invite all the Parties in the House to join hands with us in passing these Bills. The Bills are for the people. The Bills are for their welfare, their benefit. The Bills are to give power in the hands of the people. The Bills are to end the reign of the power-brokers. The Bills are to entrust responsibility to the grassroots. The Bills are to give representative administration. The Bills are to involve the people's participation in planning and implementation in development and social justice. The Bills are designed to entrench democracy in the very foundations of our polity so that the superstructure of democracy in State capitals and the national capital might be stable, sound and well-founded. The Bills represent the realisation of Mahatma Gandhi's vision. The Bills represent the fulfilment of Pandit Jawaharlal Nehru's dream. The Bills are the outgrowth of Indiraji's endeavours.

I invite the House to pass these Bills unanimously. Those who support these Bills will earn the people's gratitude. Those who oppose these Bills will fail the people and live to rue their lapse.

Annexure

1. Panchayat must be Development Oriented

   (*Inaugural address to the 13th All India Panchayat Parishad, New Delhi, 22 September, 1986 (Opening remarks translated from Hindi*)

2. Responsive and Representative Administration: Panchayati Raj

   (*Inaugural speeches at the Workshops of District Collectors and Magistrates on Responsive Administration, Hyderabad, 13 February, 1988*)

3. Focus on Panchayati Raj

   (*Free rendering of speech in Hindi while inaugurating the Panchayati Raj Sammelan of Northern States, New Delhi, 27 January, 1989*)

4. People's Participation in Planning Process

   (*Speech at the National Conference on Indian Planning Experience, New Delhi, 11 February, 1989*)

5. Democracy and Development at Doorstep

   (*Speech at the Conference of Chief Ministers on Panchayati Raj, New Delhi, 5 May, 1989*)

6. Power to the People

   (*Statement while introducing the Constitution (64th Amendment) Bill on Panchayati Raj in Lok Sabha, 15 May, 1989*)

7. Towards a Responsive and Representative Municipal Administration

   (*Address at a Seminar of Municipal Officers, New Delhi, 5 June, 1989*)

8. Demands of a Vibrant Democracy

   (Address at a Conference of Chief Ministers, New Delhi, 7 July, 1989)

9. Maximum Democracy and Maximum Devolution

   (Statement in the Lok Sabha while introducing the Constitution (65th Amendment) Bill, 7 August, 1989)

10. Dimensions of Panchayati Raj and Nagarpalika Bills

    (Text of reply to the debate on the Panchayati Raj and Nagarpalika Bills, Rajya Sabha, 13 October, 1989)

Index

Sivani
726
04/08/09